Tools for Active Christians

Tools for Active Christians

Herb Miller

The Bethany Press
St. Louis, Missouri

Scripture quotations, unless otherwise noted, are from the Revised Standard Version of the Bible, copyrighted 1946, 1952, © 1971, 1973 by the Division of Christian Education of the National Council of the Churches of Christ in the U.S.A., and are used by permission.

The scripture quotation marked TLB is taken from *The Living Bible* (Wheaton, Illinois: Tyndale House Publishers, 1971) and is used by permission.

Library of Congress Cataloging in Publication Data

Miller, Herb.
  Tools for active Christians.

  Bibliography: p.
  1. Christian leadership.   I. Title.
BV652.1.M54   254   79-14795
ISBN 0-8272-3624-7

Distributed in Canada by The G. R. Welch Company, Ltd., Toronto, Ontario, Canada

Printed in the United States of America

To Mike and Beth, greater dividends on the investment of parenthood than any father could hope for.

Contents

*"Some don't look back;
they just look confused."*

Introduction

Ninety percent of church S.O.S. calls translate into a single sentence: "Tell me how to do it." Armed with that information, leaders work hard and joyously. Minus it, commitment fades to frustration; then to disillusionment and throwing in the resignation.

Yes, some leaders need a fire of better motivation lit under their relaxed anatomy. But others just need a better idea. Jesus said, "No one who puts his hand to the plow and looks back is fit for the kingdom of God" (Luke 9:62). But some don't look back; they just look confused. Nobody told them how to lay a straight furrow in the field of their efforts.

These pages suggest the practical "how" for numerous church jobs. The ideas come from two sources: (1) congregations who developed unique solutions to specific problems and (2) countless leadership seminars conducted across the United States. They work well in some churches. Perhaps they will work in yours.

> *"The young minister quickly realized that 'reporting back' was the lynchpin to success."*

1 How Not to Let George Do It All the Time

Keys to Developing Strong Church Leaders

A young pastor arrived at his first parish with glowing enthusiasm. Passing quickly through the happy illusion stage of year one, he soon entered the grim reality phase of year two. The church's real problems now raised their heads from beneath smooth surface appearances. One of their most irritating realities was lack of money. Board meetings always received a treasurer's report. But that sheet never showed a bank balance; it only listed unpaid bills. Some months the total came to two hundred dollars, sometimes four hundred. In bad times, it reached seven hundred. When it hit a thousand, board members got worried enough to take action. Sometimes they telephoned people; sometimes they wrote pleading letters. In the most critical times, they knocked on doors or held cottage meetings.

Mortgage payments on the building provided another constant frustration. The account stood at six months behind and holding. But the sparse Sunday morning attendance disillusioned him more than anything. Looking out at vacant pews made him just plain mad, especially those of absent church offficers. Most of them weren't out of town, just out of church.

The following summer he attended a workshop where the keynoter emphasized the need for honesty. So upon arriving home, he called an elders' meeting for Sunday morning after church. They all showed up. Since he had not told them the reason for this sudden meeting, some expected him to resign. A few probably hoped so. The young pastor opened with a brief speech: "Look fellows, I am really frustrated. I'm concerned about our financial problems and our attendance problems. But do you know what irritates me most? The feeling that I'm the only person in the church who worries about these problems!"

That made a few of the officers angry. Some felt speared by the truth of it. Others thought it unfair. "We are sincerely concerned about the situation too," they protested. In that brief meeting, they did what most good church people do when confronted with a big problem. They set the time for another meeting to talk about it. But the pastor's feelings had brought a sense of urgency to the matter. They met that very Sunday night.

When the group gathered again that evening, hot anger had cooled to calm thoughtfulness. The first part of the meeting duplicated all meetings held in that congregation. They agreed with each other on all the good reasons why the church wasn't making progress. Everybody knew these six rationalizations pretty well by now. They always exchanged them at meetings, then went home feeling better. They at least *understood* the unresolvable problems they faced. "If we could just get the inactive people active. If we could get the people to give who aren't giving. If more people of our denomination would move into town." And so forth.

But this meeting ended differently. About halfway through, a realtor said, "Do you suppose we are approaching this whole problem the wrong way? Every time we have a meeting, we end up talking about what's wrong with those people out there." He pointed toward the sanctuary. "Could it be that the problem begins with us in here? Do you suppose we're expecting something to happen to other people that isn't happening to us? We are supposed to be the spiritual leaders of this church. Perhaps if we concentrated on improving our own spiritual relationship with God, the church's problems would take care of themselves."

This possibility intrigued the other men. Nobody had ever raised that idea, and it struck responsive brain cells in everyone. So they discussed it. By the meeting's conclusion, they had agreed on three basic decisions. First, they decided that they had done everything about their problems except pray about them. They hadn't thought of trying that. So they made a solemn pledge to each other that they would pray every day. They would set aside a specific time and let nothing interfere with it. During that special time each day, they would pray for each other by name. They would also pray for three other people who they thought needed God's help that week. Then they would pray for insights into their problems as church leaders.

Secondly, they pledged to read their New Testament daily. Perhaps it would shed some light on their situation. They started with Timothy and Titus, books which speak directly to church leaders. In later months, they read John's Gospel and Romans. But they began with Paul's instruction to church leaders.

12

Thirdly, they pledged to meet together once a week for one hour. Long meetings in which they discussed church problems were forbidden. These hadn't worked before. Why should they now? No, they would use the meeting time for sharing insights from their New Testament reading. Scholarly and historical approaches were ruled off limits. These methods, though excellent for Sunday school classes, would not meet their needs. Instead, they would read and underline verses that seemed to speak personally to them and their situation. The discussion leader would change each week. Each participant would take turns lifting up insights discovered in his private reading. Thus, all would take part each week on an equal basis. Every man promised that he would let nothing but an extreme emergency keep him from attending the weekly meeting.

Amazing things happened in a short time. Within two weeks, tremendous relationship changes occurred in the group. Old personality conflicts healed over. One man had always bounced everybody off the wall with his hypercritical nit-picking. His high intelligence didn't compensate for an obnoxious habit of criticizing everything and everyone. But now his speech pattern changed, and the other men began feeling differently toward him. Communication increased. The group talked openly and honestly about matters which had previously produced angry arguments. Two men from rival companies had always irritated each other. Their personality conflict was more like a two car crash. They couldn't discuss the weather without bugging each other. But now they were having congenial conversations without a tinge of animosity. They even went out to lunch together during the third week.

By the fourth week, the church's financial problems had eased. By the eighth week, they dissolved into black ink on the ledgers. But by this time that was no big deal to anyone. The other outgrowths of their experiment were far more significant. They were experiencing a new sense of peace and satisfaction in their personal lives. None of them knew about the alpha wave effect which a regular prayer life produces on the human brain. But they certainly felt themselves gaining benefits from the discipline of prayer.

Talking about Timothy and Titus eventually led them to discussing their responsibilities as shepherds in the church. So they split the congregation into separate lists of eight to ten families. Each man took pastoral responsibility for those on his list. He called on them and got acquainted. He showed a personal interest in each family member. If they were absent from worship for three consecutive weeks, the church office notified him. He could then stop by their home for a visit. He didn't browbeat them for not coming; he was just checking to see if anyone was ill. If one of his flock members entered the hospital, the church secretary automatically notified him. She also phoned him in case of a death or illness in one of his families. The members were not informed that they were on someone's list. Only the elders knew about their concern system. The apparent spontaneity of their calling seemed to add value to the process. And the personal relationships that developed between the leaders and members quickly increased the warmth of congregational life.

13

The elders soon started devoting a few minutes of each meeting to a report-back session. At that time, they discussed problems they felt merited sharing with other group members. The pastor found these moments especially helpful. An elder would say, "I called on the Browns last week. Their daughter in Denver lost her baby week before last. I'm sure nobody in the church knows about it. But I know they would really appreciate a call from you, Pastor."

Another elder might say, "Mrs. Jones is having some real headaches with her third-grade Sunday school class. I think she's about ready to give up. You might want to give her a little encouragement, Pastor. Do you think we should tell the education committee chairman? He might be able to help her solve part of her problem."

The elders vowed not to repeat these pastoral confidences to anyone, including their wives. This permitted an openness which fear would otherwise have blocked. Soon, an elder could say to his pastor, "I'm afraid they are a little upset because you didn't stop by when Jerry broke his leg. You might want to think about making a call there." The pastor could accept that direct communication from an elder who prayed for him every day. He knew it came clothed in love rather than a need to criticize.

The young minister quickly realized that "reporting back" was the lynchpin to success. The shepherding programs he had observed before all died from procrastination. But working together in a group was different. If an individual failed to function, he knew that everyone else knew about it. Together, they formed a team in which all felt their positions important. That held each player to his best in a positive way.

This group accidently rediscovered the spiritual disciplines which vitalized the New Testament church. On the day of Pentecost, three thousand converts responded to Peter's preaching. What a sermon—three thousand people flocking down the aisle for baptism. But we easily overlook what those new Christians did *after* they joined the church. Acts tells us, "And they devoted themselves to the apostles' teaching and fellowship, to the breaking of bread and the prayers" (Acts 2:42). Four simple things: They met together regularly; they studied the Bible together; they prayed together; and they extended concern for each other. Our modern group of elders accidently did the same things. So they got the same results. And any group of officers anywhere can replicate their experience, but not unless they engage themselves in the *doing* of at least those four basic things (not the talking about them, but the doing of them).

1. **Daily prayer for each other:** The pastor of the church mentioned above said, "I learned one big thing from this experience. We Christians spend too much time talking about spiritual things and too little time doing them. We are fairly rational and intelligent these days. We pride ourselves on using our minds. But this virtue sometimes leads to a terrible vice. We assume that when we have talked about a thing, we have done it. This is particularly true of prayer. We hear a sermon on prayer and think that we have prayed. Meanwhile, the prayer life of the average church officer

14

hovers somewhere between little and zero. We keep thinking we are going to start, but mostly we don't. So we don't reap the spiritual and emotional crops from it. And God can't touch us with his Spirit."

2. Daily Bible reading: Many pastors become so work overloaded that they stop reading their Bible for spiritual enrichment; they only use it as a warehouse for sermon texts and teaching material. For awhile, sermon production continues though spiritual development stops. They live off their spiritual savings account. But eventually sermon quality declines. The strength goes out of their pulpit work. Why? Because God's power doesn't reside in the material alone. The medium is definitely part of the message here. So when that human communication line shrivels, the voltage does too. Laypersons experience the same problem in a different way. Without daily digging in the roots of their faith, joy drains from church work. Congregational chores soon change into monsters, eating into personal time they resent giving. The work may go on for awhile after the motivation dies, but it won't go on well, or forever.

3. Meeting together for study and discussion: "We set a pattern which went like this," said one of the elders mentioned above. "First, we agreed not to eat. We did drink coffee, but we didn't start the rat race of bringing snacks. That only leads to culinary competition with each trying to outdo the others. Secondly, we limit our meeting time to precisely one hour. We spent about half our time talking about our New Testament readings. We used the other half to discuss our calls and concerns about people—sort of reporting in to each other. Thirdly, we closed with a brief prayer by each person."

4. Some simple system to extend concern for other church members: Lay leaders so often delegate all pastoral responsibility to the pastor. But he can't possibly get it all done. So he feels guilty (and some members help him in this self-flagellation). But even if he could do all the pastoral work, he shouldn't. People need to feel concern from each other, not just from the minister. Whatever system is developed, it must avoid loving people in abstraction. Officers can easily sit around saying, "We love everyone in the church. We are genuinely concerned about them." But does that really have any impact? Having a specific list of persons for whom you are responsible breaks up that rationalization. It makes love an active verb instead of a passive religious noun.

Three Keys to Responsible Church Leadership

Most protestant churches say they operate on democratic principles. But most fall short of democracy by not giving their members and leaders enough responsibility. Thus, members divide into two natural groups. One small segment finds joy in bureaucratic positions of power which control preachers and policies. The other large majority group practices aggressive apathy. They let all the Georges do the work. Then they periodically applaud or boo from the pew bleachers. One minister was accurately describing many congregations when he wrote on his relocation application form: "I want to be a coach in a congregation of players. I don't mind being a player as well as a coach at times. But I don't want to serve a church where I'm the only player in a congregation of coaches."

How can this situation be changed? Unlocking a safety deposit box at the bank requires two keys. One won't do it. Nor will one at a time do it. You must insert both at once. Unlocking the door to a responsible church leadership team requires three keys. And all three must function at the same time. Different churches can combine these in different ways. The congregation illustrated above is one way—certainly not the only way. But whatever pattern emerges, all three of the following keys must enter the lock simultaneously.

First, the spiritual key: Without this leaven, the whole loaf lies flat and worthless in the oven. Regardless of how much activity you stir in, little happens. You don't get fruits without roots.

Secondly, the organizational key: Small frontier churches required little organization. A group of sociologically similar people gathered from a tiny geographical circle. This small cluster constituted one of the finest support-caring systems available. Today, a vocationally diversified congregation widely separated by city miles blocks communication. Many attend two different Sunday morning services, so they rarely even see each other. Without some structured system, in this kind of situation even the best Bible study produces little real caring. Its effect is like loading a rifle cartridge with good gun powder, then forgetting to put the bullet in. The thing goes off with a loud noise, making everyone feel that something happened. But nothing has. James says, ". . .faith apart from works is dead" (James 2:26). And spiritual development programs without some kind of shepherding system are a corpse among church leaders.

The elderly constitute one obvious group which most churches neglect because of poor organizational methods. "Do not cast me off in the time of old age; forsake me not when my strength is spent," says a prayer from the Psalms (Psalms 71:9). God certainly honors that petition, but most churches do not. Ninety-five percent of post-sixty-five members living in private homes get one call a year—at the time of the annual stewardship campaign. Leaders do not *intentionally* forget God's faithful workers at the sunset of their service, but without some organized method of caring, they probably will.

Thirdly, the technical key: Training in the "how to" of such things as hospital and grief calling need not be extensive. God is more interested in our faithfulness and dedication than our methodological know-how. But commitment can not compensate for ignorance in some matters, like dealing with inactive members. If we know better, we do better. These chapters, read and discussed as a group can fill that technical vacuum.

In October of 1977, Mrs. Hartzog took forty dollars to a casino. She hit the biggest jackpot in Reno history—$246,000. Church leaders sometimes hope for that kind of magic results in their programming. They want to spend nickels of energy and get million dollar results out of God's providential slot machine. But jackpots are even more rare in church life than in Nevada. Great success is much more likely to come from getting spiritually energized, structurally organized, and technically trained.

> *"Our anxiety rings an accurate warning bell."*

2 I Wouldn't Know What to Say

How to Relate to Grief Sufferers

George Taylor fell forward into his rose garden. The massive heart attack delivered instant death. An hour later his wife, Helen, discovered him among the healthy floribundas his loving hands had brought to life.

The event was so unreal that Helen couldn't grasp it. Watching the ambulance crew gather him gently onto a rubber-tired stretcher, she felt detached. "Forty years of marriage can't end like this," she thought. "It just can't."

Friends rushed immediately to Helen's aid. Everything possible was done to help her through the grim time zone between death and funeral. A steady stream of concerned people pressed the front door bell. Most were helpful, but not all. One amputated her story of an early marriage experience with, "Don't talk about it now. Just try to think pleasant thoughts." Another presented a five-minute sermonette which could have been titled, "A Providential God Has Recalled His Creation at Just the Right Time." Another briefed her on the many happy moments she could still look forward to in life. "After all, you're still young."

Helen felt sorry for most of her awkward helpers. They just didn't understand what had happened. With a few, she felt a little angry. Her constant companion of forty years lay in a cold coffin. And she was supposed to face it with a grin?

"Fail not to be with those who weep, and mourn with those who mourn," advises an old Jewish verse from Ecclesiastes. Intuitively, we know the need for that. But isn't there something else we should do besides just be there? We want to help, to illustrate our sympathy in the moment of pain. But what, how? What if we say the wrong thing and make the tragedy worse? We feel like a blind seamstress threading a needle with bailing wire.

Our anxiety rings an accurate warning bell. The way some people relate to grief sufferers helps to ease their agony. Others, with the same good intentions, not only injure and anger; they may even extend the length of suffering. The following principles illustrate most of these wrong and right approaches. Their use requires no formal training. Just knowing what they are instantly increases our skill at helping church friends through one of life's most hurting experiences.

1. Encourage expressions of grief. Talking out grief feelings helps us accept our loss and adjust to it. Not putting grief into words and tears often results in illness later. Sometimes this is physical, like ulcers or vague chest pains that masquerade as heart ailments; sometimes it is emotional, like depression, sleeplessness, or extreme nervousness. One psychologist frequently has patients referred to him by family physicians about sixteen months after their spouse's death. Invariably, the problem is unresolved grief. They were in some way blocked from a full expression of grief when the death occurred. Now, like an embedded thorn, the anguish is working its way out through the body and mind.

Good Grief, asserted a book title on this subject. Right! The grief process helps readjust our life around the hole death shot in it. "Sorrow is better than laughter, for by sadness of countenance the heart is made glad," wrote an ancient wise man (Ecclesiastes 7:3). Instantly? No! Eventually, yes. There are definitely times when "the heart of the wise is in the house of mourning; but the heart of fools is in the house of mirth" (Ecclesiastes 7:4).

Grief will out. You can repress it for awhile. But it will eventually vent itself in some way. Much better that it explode at the right time and place than sixteen months later. By then, few friends and relatives are around to extend their love and concern. And those who do notice the pain will probably label the sufferer neurotic rather than grief-stricken. There *is* ". . .a time to mourn, and a time to dance. . ." (Ecclesiastes 3:4). And those who confuse these two times—dance when they should mourn—will probably be mourning later, at the time when they should be dancing.

2. Try to understand grief instead of being annoyed by it. Respond to the person as they feel; not the way you think they ought to feel. Some callers are upset by grief symptoms because of their own subconscious dread of death; others by their inner fear of expressing emotion. If a display of grief feelings irritates us, we should ask, "Why does this bother me?" Is it a playback of my mother's "big boys don't cry" tape from childhood days? Or is it an anxiety flashed on my mindscreen by recalling the early death of my mother? Whatever the answer, something from the storage shed of our past experiences is probably intruding into present consciousness. Only a firm commitment to "live in the present moment" can keep those past feelings from strangling our present attitudes and behavior.

3. *Don't try to blur the physical reality of death with homespun preachments.* Such sermonettes hit the mind's windshield with all the glamour of an overripe tomato. Death is very real and painful to those left alone. Like a cut on the finger, only time can dull its sharpness into a memory. So asking people to pretend it doesn't hurt equals inviting them to deny their real feelings.

Joe, the carpenter, holds a nail so Bill can hit it with the hammer. Bill misses the nail, hitting Joe's thumb. Does Joe quietly say, "Bill, that really hurts a great deal"? Unlikely.

What should Bill say in reply to Joe's yell of burnt words? "The hammer hitting your thumb was God's will. So don't feel badly about it. It was surely for the best. You just need to buck up and go on."

Unless Joe is mentally incomplete, he recognizes such language as inappropriate response to his pain and insensitivity to his feelings. In fact, if Joe was not so preoccupied with his blue finger, he would probably punch Bill in his dental work.

John and Sarah live in the same house for thirty years. They survive two years of the great depression by eating turnips, mush, and tapioca pudding. They raise three children together, rarely separated except for infrequent business trips. All grown now, the kids live in various other parts of the United States. Sarah dies of bone cancer after a brief illness, and John receives a well-meaning church caller who says, "It's a hard thing, but I know it's God's will. You'll get over it in time." Does that make sense? No, John is feeling intense pain, and intense pain is not lessened by someone telling you that it really doesn't or shouldn't hurt.

Jacob, the Old Testament patriarch, is grieving for his lost son (whom he believes to be dead). "All his sons and all his daughters rose up to comfort him; but he refused to be comforted, and said, 'No, I shall go down to Sheol to my son, mourning.' " (Genesis 37:35.) Even in this man of great faith, no words could lift his despair at the moment of his loss.

Such emotional states *always* lie beyond the influence of words. Brilliant sayings, inspirational poems, or sentence sermons about the love of God don't help. This is a time for friends to act love out by accepting the depth of the hurt; not a time to preach people out of their painful prisons. "Do not try to appease your friend in the hour of his anger or to comfort him in the hour when his dead lie before him." This old Jewish maxim from *The Sayings of the Fathers* remains sound psychology.

4. *Expect all grief to be accompanied by some degree of guilt feelings.* Twin questions walk into our mind following a loved one's death: "Should I have done something that I didn't do? Did I do something that I shouldn't have done?"

Conscience answers at least one of these in the affirmative, and we reply to ourselves with some form of "he might have lived longer if I had acted differently."

21

How do you help someone dump the guilt feelings which result from this inner dialogue? First, stifle your inclination to tell them how silly it is to feel guilty. This well-intentioned effort only blocks the guilt feelings so they can't get unloaded. Secondly, understand that since guilt is not a reasonable feeling, it can't be eradicated by logical persuasions. Thirdly, remember that with some people, pouring rational arguments on guilt is like trying to extinguish fire with gasoline. They become angry because you aren't willing to understand how they feel.

It is better to let people know that guilt is a normal part of grief. One good response is to ask *why* they feel guilty. Another is to ask what they think they should have done differently. Then listen while they tell you. That telling may stretch into several minutes. But it helps their irrational feelings to become visible to themselves.

After they finish explaining their guilt, ask them if they really think this would have lengthened the dead person's life. (This secret fear lurks below the surface of much guilt—fear that they have shortened a life.)

By this time, most can reply, "No, I guess not."

If they hesitate, continue to stress the same question in various ways: "Do you really think a different behavior would have lengthened her life?"

A twenty-two-year-old boy was referred to a psychologist by a physician. The boy's physical problems—heart palpitations, shortness of breath, tachycardia—seemed somehow related to the death of his mother. Probing for a recent stress experience, the sensitive spot was immediately located. In a rush of emotion, the boy unfolded the story of his mother's death from heart trouble. After an ambulance dash to the hospital, she remained there for nine days. During the first eight days, the boy never left her side. Dozing in a chair by the bed, he helped to turn her over during the times she felt pain and feared another attack. On the eighth day, the doctor urged the boy to go home to get some rest. She was out of danger. So he went home and slept twelve hours. During that time, his mother died of an unexpected attack. Ever since that time he had been telling himself over and over, "If I had stayed at the hospital, she would not have died."

Much listening and reality testing questions allowed Mike to get untangled from his terrible guilt. The following week his physical symptoms disappeared. No magic wand was used in the cure. Expressing guilt feelings to someone who listens without blocking our feelings often helps us find a sense of forgiveness that nothing else can.

But what if the person is really guilty? What if the guilt is real instead of false? A nineteen-year-old college student and his girl friend crossed a busy street on their way to a university stadium. Rather than walking to the light at the corner, they dashed across in the middle of the block. Teasing her with some teenage joke, he ran across the street several yards ahead of her. Reaching the far side, he turned to look back. "Betty, look out," he cried. But it was too late. The pickup truck hit hard, throwing her body several yards over the right front fender. She died of massive brain damage three days later.

"It was my fault," the boy said to a counselor. "We shouldn't have jaywalked. And I should have stayed with her."

"You're right," said the counselor. "Some responsibility for the death does fall on you. There is no way to escape that. But you have one more thing to decide. Are you going to keep on cursing yourself for the rest of your life? It is good that you admit your guilt and ask God's forgiveness. It's quite another thing to keep on discussing it with God forever. How would it be if you went out to the trash can every night and dragged out the garbage from last night to put back on the table for supper?"

"That would be stupid, I guess."

"Isn't it just as stupid to poison your mind by bringing yesterday's garbage into it every day? The Bible says that God forgives people. Do you believe that?"

"Yes."

"You are going to have to decide whether you think that is really true, or just a bunch of words. That decision is yours; nobody can make it for you."

If the person is objectively guilty (as in the above case), telling him not to think about it is a nonhelpful way of trying to be helpful. What stupid and impossible advice! Nor can you tell him that he is not guilty when he clearly is guilty. Better to be honest; then face him squarely into his responsibility for deciding how to react to his feelings.

". . .my sin is ever before me" (Psalms 51:3) perfectly describes the feelings of people hung up by the conscience collar on a nail of guilt. Why does that guilty feeling hang on so long, perhaps for years? Sometimes because grief and depression are subconscious ways of punishing ourselves for doing wrong. So we can't quit whipping ourselves until someone either tells us we are guilty (providing exterior punishment) or forgives us by listening to our story (so we can feel interior forgiveness).

5. *Expect grief to be accompanied by some anger, especially in early stages.* Sometimes this anger comes in shortlived low voltage form, invisible to onlookers. Sometimes it is extremely obvious, inappropriate, and misplaced onto innocent bystanders. It often takes the form of anger toward God: "Why has God let this happen?"

A hospital chaplain called to the emergency room met a family just arriving with an ambulance. The eight-year-old son was wheeled in D.O.A.—dead on arrival. A chunk of beef lodged in his throat had strangled him at the dinner table. This distraught mother greeted the chaplain with a curse, to which she added extensive condemnation for all other members of the cloth. Her emotional tirade continued ten minutes before she became rational.

Why did the chaplain catch it? His turned around collar cast him in the role of God's representative. At that moment, the mother was obsessed with the unfairness of this death. That, mixed with her feelings of guilt about failing to save the boy's life, made her lash out at God's lack of providential care. She later apologized and wondered why she had acted so foolishly.

The coin of grief carries anger on its opposite side. For some people, the first shock of unbearable grief is handled by turning the coin over for awhile. This form of anger is often seen at the abrupt death of a small child or the accidental death of a young adult—losses which seem so totally unfair. If the innocent bystander can understand this reflexive anger and avoid responding in kind, it soon changes back to grief.

A horrible mutation of this coin flip sometimes happens a few days after the death. A prominent woman gave leadership in her church for twenty years. Frequently elected president of the women's organization, she was loved and respected in both church and community. Her husband, a fifty-year-old banker of renown in state politics, suddenly died of a coronary. Three days after the funeral, Betty became violently angry with the pastor. Refusing to give any reason for her hostility, she stopped playing the organ and attending church. Her friends were amazed. Having known her thirty years, they had never seen her behave like this. When they sought counsel from the pastor in a nearby town, he advised waiting, listening, and continuing to give her plenty of attention and concern. The anger was slow in passing—more than a year. But Betty is back in church now, her old self again.

What happened here? For some unknown reason, Betty didn't get the grief process worked through. So she unconsciously dealt with her grief by getting mad. She didn't consciously realize what she was doing, but the anger somehow helped her to avoid facing the reality of her loss. When she was finally able to deal with her grief, she stopped being angry at the pastor.

Sometimes this unreasonable hostility is directed toward a significant lay leader. But the pastor makes a natural target. Both a symbolic representative of God and an authority figure, he is more likely than others to catch the arrow of wrath. Sometimes this irrational anger fixation passes away after a few months; sometimes it never passes. No amount of logic or persuasion by friends can move a person beyond it. They either get over it in their own good time, or they don't. While this phenomenon is rare, it usually happens to every pastor at least once in his ministry.

Such occurrences are not a big problem unless leaders fail to associate the two facts together—the death and the petty anger over a mini-matter. If they don't recognize the hostility as part of the grief, they could let a small spark blaze into a forest fire that consumes both church and pastor.

6. *Do not become so upset by the grief situation that you cannot help people.* A woman calls on a distant friend whose husband has just died. The call is pure courtesy; she has never met the husband. Nor is she really a close friend of the wife. But on greeting the bereaved widow with an embrace, she breaks into hysterical weeping. Ten minutes pass before she regains composure. During this time, the widow finds herself trying to comfort the friend who came to give *her* comfort.

Why does this happen? Different reasons for different people. A few may enjoy the attention received from a good theatrical performance. They rather like the exhibitionism of an emotional strip-tease. Others have a personality naturally predisposed to emotional expression. They cry tubs of tears at sad movies or the death of a pet goldfish. Others think that such an outpouring of emotion is the proper way to express sympathy.

Still others—overcome by the pathos and unfairness of death—empathize with those left behind. But for some people, grief situations trigger an instant replay of their own feelings from the past. Perhaps they themselves have lost a spouse, a parent, or someone close, and contact with a similar event in the present floods their mind with the exact feelings experienced at their own loss years before.

People who find these emotional overreactions to grief impossible to control should make their visits brief. This does not mean that callers should go to the opposite extreme—refuse to show any emotion at all. But they should concentrate on the needs of the bereaved, not their own needs. "Rejoice with those who rejoice, weep with those who weep," says Paul to the Romans (Romans 12:15). But balance that against his advice to the Philippians: "Let your moderation be known unto all men" (Philippians 4:5, KJV).

7. Do not try to buck them up; listen to what they are feeling. "I just don't know what to say." But you don't need to preach inspiring aphorisms to people in grief. Your physical presence helps them as much as words. Is there really anything you *can* say? You cannot promise to bring the dead person back to life, can you? And would anything short of that make the sufferer feel better? Listening 90 percent of the time and talking 10 percent probably means you are doing OK.

8. Do not divert the conversation to other subjects. Hearing the bereaved talk compulsively about the deceased sometimes raises fears in us. Are they becoming obsessed with the loss? But don't panic too soon. They will eventually finish with this phase. They won't keep on reminiscing about their mate all their life. And what better time to talk out their feelings than now? Much better than two years from now. Or worse still, having to endure unnecessary surgery or physical ailments resulting from bound up grief.

Extremely religious people sometimes try to repress their grief pain with a tourniquet of superreligiosity. One minister's wife, determined to act positive about her husband's death, reorganized the burial into a celebration. What a happy funeral! The family played joyful and brave to the capacity crowd. A year later she broke down mentally. You can't win by pretending grief doesn't hurt. The pain will somewhere, someday, some way, come out.

9. Do not fear talking about the person who died. Prepare to hear lengthy details of old memories. "The picnics we used to take" may be described at ten minute length.

"Maybe I ought to change the subject," the caller thinks. "I wonder if I'm doing something wrong?"

Probably not. As the memories come out, some of the grief pain does too. Recalling fond memories seems to put emotional anesthetic on the fresh wound.

10. Do not fear causing tears. God launders pain from the soul with salty tears. Dry cleaning won't do this job. The more water, the better. Even Jesus wept at the death of his friend (John 11:35).

11. Do not isolate people with their loneliness and loss. Relate to them. Encourage others to communicate with them. People do need aloneness at times. Be sensitive to that. But don't prejudge it. Most grief sufferers need the nearness of people more than solitude. Digging out of the grief pit is a do-it-yourself project. But the presence of people who care makes the shoveling lighter.

12. Perform some concrete act. Pies and fried chicken start arriving immediately. "What a waste," critics may say. "They won't eat that for a month. This mob of people bringing food won't let them get any rest."

If food alone was needed, McDonalds could solve it more conveniently. But much more than calories flow through the front door—the reassuring presence of caring people. The grieving don't need rest as much as the knowledge that they are not alone.

Flowers at the funeral serve the same purpose. They paint a picture that says, "somebody cares." Many families wish to divert the money to meritorious funds instead. Such charity provides an excellent alternative. But flower gifts still smell sweet long after they wilt. Not for the deceased, but for those left behind.

13. Stay alert for symptoms of physical illness. Grief stresses the physical to its outer limits. So watch for health problems resulting from such stress, especially in the elderly. If in doubt, call their physician. In this instance, friends should stop listening and start giving orders. Take charge. Tell them exactly what to do.

14. After the initial shock has passed, encourage them to keep busy. Involve them in activities with other people. "I don't think I'll ask her to go," the neighbor said. "Joe only died three weeks ago. She probably wouldn't feel like it."

Wrong! Busyness is not happiness, but it's the next best substitute. Don't force participation in social events. Grown people generally know what they don't or do enjoy. But don't assume that "she would rather be alone for awhile." The flood of phone calls and friends soon diminishes to a trickle. The physical exhaustion quickly passes. The need for solitude vanishes shortly after the funeral. When the loud sound of emptiness sets in, congregational activities help to compensate.

15. Loneliness is often more acute three months later than three days after the funeral. Church people are extremely helpful the first week after a death, and fair the second week. But after fourteen days, only a few close friends remember it happened. "She'll work it out," they think. She does. But that takes a long time. So save some of your concern for later.

Widows and widowers face one big stress that few people notice. They sit with their husband or wife in a certain pew for years. Sitting down in that place the first time after the death, they become terribly conscious of the empty seat beside them. Memory journeys them back to other years. They see not only the spouse, but children sitting nearby. Floods of memories bring floods of unexpected feelings. Considerate friends can invite the bereaved to attend church with them the first time or two. Completely eliminate the emptiness? No, but it takes the sharp edge off the pain.

26

Church leaders should work out systematic ways to extend concern over a period of several months. "He heals the brokenhearted, and binds up their wounds." (Psalms 147:3.) Right. Only *he* can do it. We cannot. But God does much better surgery if his church helpers assist.

16. Try to understand unresolved grief. What if several years pass and the grief remains? A big bundle of guilt is the most likely explanation. Mr. and Mrs. Sims stopped attending church three years ago. After their son was killed in a freak auto accident during basic training, they never came back. Mr. Sims became angry at the time of the funeral. "Thoughtless behavior" was the phrase he used to describe the pastor's attempt to be helpful.

But the next pastor eventually learned from a friend that Mr. Sims and his son had been on poor terms. In fact, those poor terms had caused the boy to run away from the family farm to join the army. Mr. Sims has been blaming himself for the death ever since.

The pastor in another church visited all his members after arriving at his new parish. Conscientiously calling on the inactive members too, he was greeted warmly by Mrs. Lindsay. After accepting the customary cup of coffee, he began with the usual questions about her background and family. Three minutes into the conversation he encountered a flood of grief regarding her late husband. The tears flowed freely as she talked, making him glad he had come. She was lonely. He wished the secretary had told him of her recent loss; he would have called sooner.

After listening sympathetically to several minutes of explanation about not coming to church because she missed him so much, the pastor asked, "How long ago did you lose him?"

"Nine years ago this summer," she replied with a new burst of tears.

Pastor Smyth knew she wasn't telling the whole story. She had tremendous unresolved grief, but why? A year passed before he found the answer. Calling on Mrs. Lindsay's neighbor, also a church member, he got the information by accident. Mr. and Mrs. Lindsay's marital conflicts had been the talk of the town. "She chased him out of that house and down the street with a shotgun one time," the neighbor said. "Another time she followed him out on the front porch with a big butcher knife. A couple of times the neighbors called the sheriff. With all that screaming they thought somebody was getting murdered."

Not all unresolved grief originates with guilt feelings, but 90 percent probably does. In another church, Mrs. Carnagie constantly brought up the death of her son-in-law two years ago. When church friends called, she invariably shifted the topic to his death. Since the Carnagies had only recently moved to that community, nobody could understand why.

But when old friends of the Carnagies moved to town and joined the same church, the rest of the story emerged. Mrs. Carnagie had been violently opposed to her daughter's marriage—had practically disowned the girl for marrying him. For a time, she refused to have them in her home. Then the boy was shipped overseas—to Vietnam. The second month there, he was blown to pieces by a land mine. And Mrs. Carnagie was left with the bitter memory of her rejection.

Unresolved grief occasionally produces an unusual phobia. Mrs. Sargeant came back to church for the first time after her husband's death. Each time she looked toward the front of the sanctuary, she saw his casket there. She smelled flowers. She didn't go back to worship for several weeks. When she went back the second time, it happened again. Several years pass; it still happens each time she returns to church. The problem has now developed into a full-scale phobia—a church attendance phobia. Such problems are very difficult to overcome (as are all phobias). No amount of logic or willpower removes that vision from her head—and the subsequent flood of emotion it triggers.

How do such phobias originate? The human mind is like a ten story building full of offices full of file cabinets full of file folders. In these folders (brain cells) are stored all past feelings and experiences. Most of these feelings and memories cannot be recalled at will. We know they exist, for they can be summoned by hypnosis. But for some people, similar sights, smells, and sounds call them up too. It's as if a crazy little file clerk runs through the hallways of our mind, getting into the wrong file cabinet. Then he pulls out the wrong file folder and slaps it on the desk top of our consciousness. And suddenly we feel exactly the same as we did the day of the funeral. Fortunately, psychologists now treat this difficulty quickly and successfully. Unfortunately, few sufferers know that. So they don't seek professional help.

17. Organize a system of continuing contact and concern. "Pure religion and undefiled before God and the Father is this, To visit the fatherless and widows in their affliction. . . ." (James 1:27, KJV.) One rural church takes this seriously. Under their "adopt a widow" program, each church officer takes responsibility for a specific widow. During winter months, this involves a daily phone call to be sure she is OK; helping with fix-it projects; providing transportation for church events in bad weather.

Whatever the system, break the total church membership into lists assigned to specific officers. Every grief sufferer thus becomes the responsibility of a specific leader. This puts the emphasis on continuing care rather than Band-Aid help at the time of death. It also gives authentic meaning to the phrase "the church is the *family* of God."

In the movie *Oh God,* George Burns (who plays God) appears to John Denver in his bathroom. In the animated conversation that follows, John Denver says to God, "Everything is such a mess down here. We need more help. Why don't you help us more?"

George Burns adjusts his horn-rimmed glasses and replies, "That's why I gave you one another."

3 My Aunt Hattie Had That Same Thing

How to Visit Hospital Patients

The patient breathed hard behind his oxygen mask. As the church caller made small talk, he began to gasp for air. Frightened, the caller pushed the buzzer to summon a nurse. The patient pointed wildly toward the bedside table. Seeing a pencil and pad there, the visitor handed them to him. Frantically scribbling something on the paper, he handed it back to the caller. But just as the paper touched his fingertips, the patient collapsed. The nurse arrived two seconds later and waved him out of the room. "I'm sorry," she said. "He's dead."

Thrusting the paper into his pocket, the caller forgot about it. But while talking with the widow, who arrived twenty minutes later, he remembered. "Here," he said. "I'm sure he would want you to have this. They were his last words."

The grief-stricken wife unfolded the paper and read, "You are standing on my oxygen tube."

Most church callers aren't quite that clumsy. But many are fearful of doing or saying something wrong. "I want to show my concern," said one elder. "But how can I be sure that my call will be helpful?" Such fear is realistic. Here, as in grief calling, knowing positive principles helps us stay off emotional oxygen hoses.

1. Assume that the call should be made. People need a call from the pastor. But they also desire calls by church friends. The pastor brings the fresh breeze of God's love. But lay people communicate people love. Patients need both. So neither call can replace the other.

"Be not slow to visit the sick," says an old Jewish proverb from Ecclesiastes. In his parable about sheep and goats, Jesus adds a spiritual dimension to that practical suggestion (Matthew 25:31-46). "Calling on the sick equals calling on me," he tells us. "And failure to make sick calls could even cause an 'F' on your final exams."

Are there ever times when we shouldn't call? Wait three days after any major surgery. Until then, flowers are better company than people. The only other exception is personal antagonism between caller and callee. Some church people relate like two pieces of sandpaper. Such nonfriends seldom make positive hospital calls. And this is certainly not the time to work out differences. So don't be overcome with guilt and rush down to make things straight. A hospital stay is poor timing for a peace conference.

With these two exceptions, any member can make a good call. Here again, develop a simple system to back up the haphazard calls of friends. Each elder or officer should carry responsibility for certain families. A phone call from the church secretary notifies the officer. Thus, nobody gets out of the hospital without at least one call from a church friend.

2. Knock before entering. Even if the door is ajar, knock and wait for a verbal invitation to enter. Encountering the patient undressed or on the bedpan adds unredeemable awkwardness to the visit.

3. A light above the door indicates that a nurse has been called. Some hospital procedure may be in progress. If uncertain about this, check the nurses' station. They can advise whether it is permissible to enter. Nurses appreciate such consideration. Don't be intimidated by apparent exceptions, like those with the "older nurse syndrome." Such gruff exteriors are sometimes seen in veterans of many years experience (rarely in younger nurses). They have spent years dealing with pain, tight schedules, complaining patients, and irritating relatives. So they develop an armor-plated exterior and vitriolic tongue as self-defense. Don't believe what you read on his or her face. The exterior packaging protects a warm heart from getting mangled in the pressure cooker of hospital routine.

4. See yourself as the patient's guest. Anyone paying such high rent on such a small space should get to use it the way he or she wishes. Is the patient asleep? Don't awaken him. He likely needs rest more than company. A note left on the bedside table announces your good intentions. Nor is it helpful to stand by and watch her eat dinner. Even hungry pets are often too embarrassed to eat while someone is staring at them. Avoid carrying strong odors into the room, like pizza, onions, or loud perfume. The patient's nauseated stomach may be acutely offended. Don't carry colds or a virus to hospitals. Telephone and explain why you can't come. The patient will appreciate your thoughtfulness in staying home.

Respect hospital rules. A nurse ran nineteen guests out of a teenager's room which had a "no visitor" sign on the door. Throwing a party was a thoughtful gesture, but of questionable therapeutic value. Is the room already crowded with visitors? Be bright, be brief, and be gone.

5. Stand facing the patient. As a result of surgery or broken bones, some patients have limited radius of eye and neck movement. The unthinking visitor who sits in a chair by the head of the bed easily turns his eyes toward the patient. But how frustrating for the patient unable to return the glance.

Where is the window in this room? Are the drapes drawn or open? Is the patient squinting at your face against a screen of blinding sunlight? If possible, take a standing position halfway to the bed's foot. Thus, the patient looks you in the eye without performing neck and pupil contortions. Do not take a seat until invited.

Suppose the room contains two beds, and your patient lies farthest from the door, by the window. Without thinking, you move to a position between the two beds. Bad tactical error! These two roommates know each other well by now. So your patient introduces you to her friend. Natural chitchat begins. But how do you terminate this three-way conversation? Hard to break off without seeming rude, isn't it?

If you walk immediately to the outside of the farthest bed, introductions still happen. But four yards of distance make three-way discussions unnatural. So after acknowledging the introduction, you can resume a private conversation without awkwardness. This allows the patient to talk to you about things which she may not wish to broadcast publicly.

6. Use caution in physical contacts with the patient. Super-salesman handshakes can give physical pain to postoperatives, heart patients, or mending broken ribs. Let him initiate the handshake. Then be gentle.

Don't sit on the bed. As well as bringing physical discomfort to some patients, germs accumulated on clothing fabric can transfer to linens. Then too, people bedfast for long periods begin to experience the bed as a personal part of their body. Visitors rarely enter a private home and sit down on the hostess's lap. Similarly, bed perching is felt by some patients as an uninvited imposition on their body space.

Some nervous visitors don't know what to do with their hands. So they fiddle with the blanket, smooth the sheets, or drum their fingers to a march cadence on the bed railing. This feels about as pleasant to the patient as having someone tap-tapping on her anklebone.

7. Be brief. One pastor of a small church stays two hours on hospital calls. His members consequently try to get in and out of the hospital without him finding out. They can stand the surgery, but can't tolerate his long visits.

Fifteen minutes is plenty. For the extremely ill, less is better. Watch for signs of tiredness—yawning, twisting tissues, or difficulty making conversation. Don't misconstrue the patient's "I wish you could stay longer" as an accusation of neglect. This parting remark is usually just a courteous expression of appreciation for the call.

8. *Feel the patient's emotional pulse and fit your mood to hers*. She may be ready to crack jokes. The doctor just made rounds and told her, "You can go home tomorrow." On the other hand, she may be in the most serious mood of her life. The doctor just gave her the terrifying news, "You have a malignancy." Charging in like a clown and telling her the latest traveling salesman joke is about as funny as a rubber aspirin.

Check her mood state. Follow her lead. This doesn't require psychiatric training. Just be sensitive to her voice, facial expressions, and conversational pattern. She'll let you know. In doing this it is usually best, however, to avoid asking the patient to label her illness. What if the problem happens to be one of those sexual maladies whose description causes embarrassment? "How are you feeling?" makes a better beginning. "How are things going?" is another good way to start. Patients can then tell you their problem and prognosis if they wish. Usually, they do, providing you give them a chance. So don't interrupt with illustrations of similar medical cases you have heard about in other people.

9. *Listen to the patient's feelings*. He needs someone to listen to his feelings; not someone to lecture him on how he should feel by now, or how he will feel when he gets better. He may not be better *now*. So meet him where he is, not where you wish he was. If his spirits are in the cellar, you will do more to move him upstairs by listening than by quipping, "Oh, you'll soon be fine." Such optimistic patter blocks him from further talk. But listening to his hurts and fears helps reduce their weight. Fearful feelings can get trapped in whirlpools of the brain. Until someone lets out the poison gas by listening, faith and hope can't get in.

A patient suffering anxiety following a serious heart attack said, "I'm afraid I'll never leave the hospital."

His visiting friend replied, "Oh, you mustn't say that. You'll soon be up and out of here. Just don't think about it. You have a good doctor."

A far better reply would have been, "What makes you say that?" The patient could then have reduced his fear by telling it to someone. Or the visitor could have said, "You feel that you are too sick to get well?" Such a question always signals the willingness to listen to feelings and fears.

The three magic words "You feel like. . ." followed by a rephrasing of the patient's last sentence is always a good way to encourage continued expression of feelings.

A patient suffering extreme pain said, "I just don't see why God is making me go through this."

The visitor replied, "Oh, I don't think God causes people to suffer. That's not the way God is."

The visitor should have said, *"You feel like God hasn't been fair to you."* If she had, the patient would have kept on talking and would probably have talked himself out of the way he felt.

Another good listening technique is simply repeating the last two or three words of the sentence the patient just said. Used with a questioning voice inflection, this generally causes the patient to continue. A bit irritating if used constantly, such a habit is rarely noticed if used only occasionally.

Whatever listening method you use, visualize yourself as a mirror instead of a brain full of witty advice. Reflect her feelings rather than trying to overcome them with rational arguments. In this context, the ear has more power than the mouth. This doesn't mean that a visitor should never reassure. It just means that reassurance must not be offered too soon. When the patient starts reassuring you, it is time to agree with her.

10. Don't diagnose. "How are you feeling?" Joe begins.

Martha describes her ailment.

Joe's computer spins when he hears the medical words. A relative who had that same problem pops into his consciousness. "My Aunt Hattie had that," he interjects.

"How did she get along?" the patient naturally inquires.

Joe sees the conversational quicksand too late. Not wanting to tell a lie, he says, "She got better for awhile, but she eventually died."

Joe's comment introduces a medically inaccurate fear to Martha's mind. Two patients can carry the same diagnostic label, but a radically different prognosis for recovery. Similar illnesses take many different forms and outcomes.

A family physician asked the chaplain to see a hospital patient. "Her respiratory problem is serious, but certainly not fatal," the doctor said. "The real problem is that she has decided she is going to die. I can't seem to shake her from it. If we don't change her mind, she will die."

Two hours of listening later the chaplain finally unraveled the mystery. An inhalation therapist had accidently made the "Aunt Hattie Mistake." While giving her respiration therapy with a portable machine, the two had chatted. The patient, proud of remembering the big diagnostic term the doctor had given her that morning, described her ailment. The therapist shared the story of her aunt—same diagnosis—who died within a few months. That patient, a person of high anxiety anyway, had concluded that her doctor was protecting her from the full implications of her diagnosis.

An active churchman was recovering from malignant colon surgery. On hearing the story of his long ordeal, a visitor responded with, "Oh my God, that will kill you. My brother died of that exact same thing two years ago. In fact, I have a close friend dying in the hospital at Big Spring, Texas, with that same thing right now. And I have an aunt in Peoria, Illinois, who has it. They say she won't live 'til Christmas."

To this heartening news the patient protested, "Well, my doctor says that she got it all. I should get completely well."

"Oh, they will always tell you that," the cheerful visitor responded. "They know if they tell you the truth you will give up. Believe me, you are really in trouble."

11. Avoid giving advice. One cancer patient entertained many compulsive advice givers during his weeks of hospitalization. "You look much better than you did a week ago," some would say. "Maybe you ought to get up and walk more." During that time he had lost ten pounds, and his temperature was two degrees higher than the week before. Rather than encouraging him, their comments made him suspect that he was being

33

deceived. Perhaps vital information was being withheld about his condition!

Other visitors would come in the very same day and tell him, "You really look bad. Maybe you shouldn't be walking so much. You might overexert yourself." This observation was more accurate, but equally nonhelpful.

Still others advised, "You ought to get another doctor on the case. Dr. Johnson really helped my aunt. It wouldn't hurt to get another opinion you know. You don't want to just lie here and die." This really helped increase his confidence in his physician.

Don't give medical advice of any kind unless you write M.D. after your name. And even then, not unless this patient is your patient.

12. *Avoiding bringing up family problems caused by her absence.* "I'll bet those kids will be glad to have you home," said one visitor. Attempting to make the mother feel loved, he only made her feel guilty and uneasy. She started thinking of home duties which needed her attention.

"I was by the house last night visiting with Gene," said an elder to another woman. "They'll sure be glad to have you home. That house is really a mess." He was trying to help her feel needed. But he sentenced her to lie there looking at the ceiling for seven more days, visualizing the chaos in her living room.

Nor should the visitor speak glowingly of how smooth things are running without her, especially with patients hospitalized for lengthy stretches. If things are going so beautifully in her absence, she may easily start thinking, "I guess they don't really need me anymore." Such thought patterns do little to improve recovery rates.

Better to avoid statements on how good or gross things are at home. Construct small talk about mutual friends, world events, and community affairs. Discuss the home situation if the patient leads that way. But don't superimpose this subject because you know it is close to her heart. It may be too close.

13. *Don't talk in the presence of sleeping or unconscious patients.* The terminally ill often retain the facility of hearing long after they appear unconscious. And patients in a semicomatose condition frequently hear every word said in the room. So don't whisper in their presence. Always step out in the hall.

A visitor asked one relative, "How is he doing?"

The relative replied, "The doctor says he probably won't make it. Only has about a 10 percent chance. It will probably be a couple of days at the most."

But the patient lived. Later, he reported hearing the conversation and feeling angered by it. There he lay, trapped alone in his body, unable to move or speak, with this good news to ponder.

Stroke victims are particularly vulnerable to this carelessness. Their hearing is not impaired; their mind is clear. They simply cannot talk, move, or respond to what they hear. Since many relatives are not aware of this, visitors should take the initiative in avoiding inappropriate conversation. If a family member starts loudly volunteering all the bad news, say, "Let's go out in the hall." Turn and lead the way, or take them by the arm.

The surgical patient working through the hours of recovery from anesthesia has patches of time when she hears perfectly but can't move. Unsuspecting visitors and relatives waiting beside the bed should therefore avoid discussion of what the doctor said about the surgery.

A minister recovering from a bad auto accident overheard a conversation between two visitors. One said to the other, "Poor soul, he isn't going to last very long. He'll be gone within a day or so at most."

The minister didn't know they weren't talking about him. "It sure gave me a jolt," he said. "It was several days before I found out differently."

Even with conscious patients, don't congregate in whispering groups outside their door. Patients usually assume that whispers are guarded conversation regarding their dark prospects for recovery. Get far enough away so that muffled conversation cannot be misinterpreted as attempts to withhold bad news.

14. If the patient shows anger toward you or others, don't overreact or try to pry. Ill people often develop strong feelings of unreasonable fear or anger. All adults act childish and immature at times. But since the hospital patient is treated like a child, these regressions to infantile thinking patterns are more common. Placed in a totally dependent role—confined to his room—waited on hand and foot—told what he shall and must not eat—separated from his clothing and dressed in pajamas—run like a half-naked sheep through various rooms and machines in a robe which barely conceals his backside—such treatment would aggravate a healthy person, much less a sick one. Drugs and poor physical condition can also increase the childishness. Added to this, a long-term patient has ceased his productive role at home and work. He thus loses much of the self-esteem which makes everyone feel like a worthwhile adult.

Patients bedfast for several weeks are prone to a period of mental depression. During this one or two week period of low spirits, some feel that they have lost their faith: They can't pray; they can't feel the love of God; they have lost all hope, feel worthless, and sometimes think of suicide.

Trying to talk people out of this blue low with logical reason rarely helps. Nor do jokes and funny stories lift such moods. The depressed person may even seethe with anger at joking efforts to lift her altitude. To her, the visitor appears to be saying, "Cheer up. Your feelings are not a problem because they aren't really there. Don't be such a burden to us by feeling despondent."

The family usually responds by thinking, "What are we doing wrong? We must not be taking good care of her or she wouldn't feel that way." But the family can do little to either prevent this low or help the patient get through it. Fortunately, this condition, like the measles, is self-limiting. It eventually passes, regardless of what measures are used. But bystanders can rarely hasten its completion.

Several natural causes produce this depression. The physical inactivity of lying in bed for several weeks causes a physiological reaction that affects mood. In spite of her attempt to maintain a positive mental outlook, out-of-balance hormone systems will warp her rational thinking ability. Relatives and friends should therefore avoid blaming her and telling her to "Shape up your attitude and stop feeling sorry for yourself." Such advice is like saying to a sugar diabetes victim that he will be OK if he gets a better attitude.

Illness-induced depressions arise partly from the fact that the individual has stopped producing. Without realizing it, he has viewed himself as a worthwhile person because of his many worthwhile activities. Now, like all aged or handicapped people, he must reorganize his self-identity. Seeing himself as a person of value simply because he *exists* takes some rethinking time.

Human creatures operate best when goal oriented. Remove daily goals for long periods, as in hospitals and prison camps, and depression almost always results. This reaction is much worse in the elderly patient, for whom life may hold few future goals, even if she recovers. Freud seems correct in defining mental health as *lieben und arbeiten* (love and work). Absence of either ingredient creates sad individuals. Eric Sevareid said in one of his last broadcasts before retirement, "People need three things: security, identity, and stimulation." A bedfast person has security (unless he is terminally ill). But he loses his identity as a contributor to the world. And he loses the stimulation of life participation. Some other sage has observed that happiness involves three things: something to do, someone to love, and something to look forward to. However you package a happiness definition, lying in a bed doesn't meet the qualifications.

Depression may be a natural coping mechanism. Like grief, it may allow the individual to pull himself into a cocoon for awhile, until he can adjust to a new reality. So don't argue with patients about religion or anything else. Never return hostility for hostility. Listen and ask questions. Assume that depressive or angry states are a temporary condition. Take Paul's advice to the Romans: "We who are strong ought to bear with the failings of the weak. . ." (Romans 15:1).

15. Don't prejudge the patient's religious needs. Brief prayers are almost always acceptable. But seek her permission first. "I'd better be running along now. Would you like me to have a word of prayer with you before I go?"

What kind of prayer? If possible, avoid reciting from books or memory. Catch up the patient's mood. Form reflection pools of prayer from feelings she has expressed or implied. Pray for rest during this night (patients often sleep poorly)—for those who care for us here—for those we love—for God's healing power—whatever seems natural.

Patients occasionally say no to prayer offers. Don't take this rejection personally. Such refusals don't mean you have failed in your visiting. Good, but perhaps not obvious reasons, may exist to explain why he is not in the mood to talk with God. "I certainly understand" or "That's fine; perhaps another time" allows you to depart without embarrassment. Don't ask the patient *why* he doesn't wish to pray. This drives him into a defensiveness which concludes the call on a negative note.

Avoid sermonettes, either in prayers or conversation. Leave the preaching to preachers. If she wants a sermon, she can flip on the TV, get the Del Rio radio station, or read *Guideposts*.

16. Don't use hospital visits for evangelism purposes. Every small hospital has at least one self-appointed "God's Little Helper." These freelance gurus visit patients of all religious affiliation. Poor ethical conduct and bad religious etiquette, such efforts seldom convert people. Patients often draw closer to God while in the hospital, but not because of bedpan evangelists. Withdrawal from their hectic life-style gives time for calm reflection—time to think of life's priorities—sometimes of life's sure outcome, death. Silence, more than sermons, aids this meditation.

17. Complete isolation from visitors is often the first and best form of treatment for the emotionally ill. During the first three weeks, sometimes longer, some psychiatrists prohibit all visitors. Eliminating all contact with previous relationships seems to wipe the brain's blackboard clean, allowing patients to reconstruct a fresh slate. Mothers of such patients may respond in irritation, "That doctor won't even let *me* in to see her. Why, she is my daughter. I don't see what he thinks I would do to her."

The mother needs assurance that she isn't being tagged as a bad parent. The psychiatrist isn't implying that. He simply knows from long experience with this kind of patient that early isolation will probably reduce the hospital stay by several weeks.

Many psychiatrists ban all pastors and church callers for the entire time of hospitalization. Bibles and religious literature are often barred from the ward. Such restrictions should not be viewed as antireligious, but as pro health. The spiritual blackboard, as well as the emotional dimension, needs erasing. Then too, false guilt feelings accidently aroused by the sight of church friends can sometimes inhibit the unraveling of psychological problems.

Length of stay in a psychiatric ward often runs to six weeks. While this seems long to relatives, it does not signify incurable illness. Many patients emerge permanently well.

18. Understand the stages through which terminally ill patients pass when facing death. Should the patient be told he is dying? A moot question, since he almost always senses the truth anyway. Either through self-awareness or unconscious hints dropped by relatives, he knows.

John Harding received a cancer diagnosis following surgery. His wife, Martha, decided that they shouldn't tell him. His health gradually deteriorated. Multiple cobalt treatments sapped his strength and appetite. He lost weight and eventually died. They never did tell him the facts. John and Martha had lived together in truthfulness for forty years. But during the last year of his life, they lived a lie. John soon sensed that she was not telling him everything. So he tried to keep her from knowing that he knew she was lying. And she tried to keep him from seeing that she knew that he knew. This deception was forced on other family members. Against her will, the pastor was involved in the lie. So during the last weeks of his life, John suffered terrible aloneness. He had nobody to talk with about his feelings. Because everyone was sworn to secrecy, so was he. A timid and sensitive man, he never had the courage to tell them that he knew he was dying. That would have been like telling them they had failed to protect him from the painful knowledge.

This experience happens with less frequency now than one or two decades ago, mostly because doctors have become more willing to deal with death. Repeated studies among physicians indicate an abnormal fear of death. After all, a dying patient proves failure of the healing art. So admitting that the patient is dying would involve facing your failure to save him. Then too, admitting death's approach might force the doctor to talk with the patient about it, a most uncomfortable procedure. This fear is so great that in one 600 bed hospital nobody would admit to the existence of a single terminally ill patient. Fortunately, current health care people hold increasingly realistic attitudes toward the dying patient.

Medical exceptions do, of course, exist which would restrict a doctor from telling a patient about death. One cancer patient also had a serious heart ailment. The knowledge of her condition might have triggered an earlier death by heart attack. At this point, one rule stands taller than all others: Visitors must abide by the physician's decision and the will of close family members.

Emotional Stages Preceding Death

If the dying person lives long enough, he passes through five emotional stages on his way to death. If the end comes too quickly, he may not experience all of them. The process may be abbreviated at stage two or three, but at least part of these phases can be observed in all terminally ill patients. A much more thorough explanation of these well known stages has been given by Dr. Elisabeth Kubler-Ross in her book *On Death and Dying* (Macmillan Company, 1969).

1. Denying death. "Not me!" describes the characteristic conversational phrase and emotional feeling. The person rejects the idea of death. "No, it can't be me!" On hearing his doctor announce his approaching death, one strong-minded athlete said, "I'm going to whip this thing." The certain diagnosis of bone cancer throughout the body was shoved into the mental background. That couldn't happen to him. He was a winner, not a loser. He eventually faced the truth, but not until several days later.

2. Anger at death. "Why me??!!!" describes the conversational and thought pattern. Sometimes the anger is directed at God. "This isn't fair. I've attended church all my life. I've tithed my money. I've worked hard for the church. Why would God do this to me?"

3. Bargaining with death. "Me, but not yet," describes the thought pattern of this stage. "Yes, Lord, it is me. But couldn't you wait 'til after

38

Susie's wedding next summer? Couldn't it be after Jerry's graduation? I'll give a large memorial gift to the church if you let me live until Christmas." Much praying may occur in this stage, pleading with God to put off the disaster.

4. Depression. "It is me!" describes the thought pattern. Facing this harsh reality inevitably turns on the emotional coping mechanism of depression, or blues. Those who arrive here know the meaning of the old phrase "dark night of the soul."

5. Acceptance and adjustment. Movement to this final stage does not always occur in the exact order described. Circumstances sometimes scramble sequence. But stage five is always last. "Yes, me" describes the mental pattern. Emotional and spiritual peace comes at last. Those who arrive here illustrate the greatest height to which the human spirit can rise. The patient feels ready to face with faith and courage the cessation of his own existence. Pastors who have repeatedly observed this behavior find themselves inspired anew each time. What marvelous capacities God has given us! We can even meet our own death face to face and feel at peace.

Can we help people pass through these stages more quickly? Not much. But just knowing that the stages exist helps some. That keeps us from getting quite so upset during the bad spots—keeps us from blaming ourselves for how they feel—keeps us from getting tangled up in their emotional ball of yarn. Knowing the stages helps us to act more normal around them, which is what they most need from us.

One of the best things we can do is be present. We can call on them. We can spend time with them. We can avoid avoiding them because we don't know what to say. Death washes your mind with the ultimate loneliness. At the trauma of birth, you find some comfort in other people. But when you die, you die alone, even in a crowd. Nobody can go with you down that road. But having friends there at the cloverleaf helps a little. Especially friends you know will continue to love the loved ones you leave behind.

Dying persons sometimes ask friends and relatives to assist in tidying up final affairs. "I'd like for you to get those salt shakers out of the cedar chest and give them to Julie. She is my only granddaughter, and I want her to have them."

If such an act is ethical and legal, do it. Don't say, "Oh, you'll be up and around soon. You can do that yourself one of these days." Such remarks are shallow helpfulness in the deep water of death.

On the other hand, people can become unreasonable and irrational at some stages of their adjustment. So be careful what promises you make. They may ask you to clear something up with an old enemy. They may request something that you have no authority to do. Don't make rash unkeepable promises that leave you feeling guilty later. "It's natural for you to want me to do that, and I'll do what I can," one friend answered in that kind of situation. "But you must understand that I may not be able to succeed at it."

Try to treat dying people normally. Avoid constructing a cocoon or superficial unreality for their last days. Difficult? Yes, because watching a friend face death frightens us. Standing at her elbow forces us to lift the protective lid of unreality from *our own* terminal stage. Each of us sails through life on the operating principle, "I am never going to die. Other people die, but I don't. I am eternal." But watching a friend's death cracks the foundations of that illusion. "If they die, perhaps I can die too." None of us wish to admit that to ourselves.

The movie *Oh God* ends with God, played by George Burns, appearing in a final courtroom scene. He has to show up in order to prove that his prophet, a frightened supermarket manager played by John Denver, is not crazy. After a dramatic display of card tricks, God makes himself invisible and walks out. Only the noise of his squeaking tennis shoes marks his movement toward the creaking swinging doors before the judge's bench. Then he squeaks toward the back of the courtroom. As the great double doors swing shut, he closes his presence by saying, "Try not to hurt each other. There's been enough of that." Double that advice for hospital callers.

4 Extinguishing Church Fires

How to Deal with Angry Church Members

Phil's hands shook as he opened his car door in the church parking lot. He had never seen anyone get that mad before. Harry, the Sunday school superintendent, had stopped him in the hall after church. Face red, voice trembling, he exploded in a Vesuvian irritation. The subject matter of his anger made no rational sense. Why would a grown man get so mad just because the Lord's Prayer had not been used in the worship service?

Rare is the church leader who doesn't at some time deal with a hopping mad member. They may think the preacher has done something to them. They may feel that the church, or a board chairman, has done them dirt. *Something* has gone wrong. They are red in the face, redder in speech, and appear ready to hurt somebody violently.

This is one of those times when "A word fitly spoken is like apples of gold in a setting of silver" (Proverbs 25:11), and "neither deadly poison nor sharp-whetted sword is as fatal as the ill-spoken word" (Buddhist saying from the *Jataka*). But how do you speak a fit word to a person in that kind of mood? Are there any procedures that help in such situations? Yes, the same set of principles used by experts in the business world or other settings.

1. Isolate them. If they accost you in a busy hallway, get them to a more private spot. That at least stops their hot words from starting accidental

41

brushfires of discontent in bystanders. "I'd like to hear your opinions about that. Here, let's go into this classroom and talk about it." If feasible, say, "Let's go get a cup of coffee and talk about it."

2. Get them to sit down someplace. Most people find it much harder to stay angry sitting down than standing up. So just getting them seated may cut their anger in half. (Not only that, they can't punch you so hard from a sitting position.) The angry person subconsciously seeks a fight with somebody. Early caveman reflexes take over. Adrenal systems organize him for a wild animal skirmish. Sitting down helps reverse the physiological trends of this fighting mood. The emotional and illogical thought process so necessary in a good fight are slowed. Adrenaline levels decelerate. Blood pressure, heart rate, and breathing rapidity decline toward normal.

Talk to the angry person slowly, calmly, and quietly (even if your own heart pounds with anxiety). "A soft answer turns away wrath, but a harsh word stirs up anger," observed someone long ago (Proverbs 15:1). And that is especially true for those who deal with angry people. Another world religion puts it this way: "Activity overcomes cold; inactivity overcomes heat; so the wise man by his calm sets everything right in the world" (a saying of Taoism from the *Tao-Teching*). Psychologists have now validated these maxims experimentally. A soft, quiet voice, with slow-moving speech tranquilizes the conversational partner. Without knowing it, the person coming on like a downhill freight train begins to speak more calmly. Consequently, he starts thinking more calmly.

3. Listen carefully. Zip your mouth. Let her talk. Time is on your side. The more she talks, the faster she will run down. Few people can stay hopping mad for many minutes. Hopping is too emotionally and physically tiresome. So encourage her to cleanse her venom system. Ask questions to let her clarify her position. "Let me be sure that I know what you mean. Do I understand correctly that you feel like. . . ." Repeating her feelings in your own words helps her to know that you are listening.

4. Tell him that you agree with some specific part of what he has said. Perhaps you agree with the principle he is defending, or perhaps you agree with a minor point, but agree with something. Don't be dishonest. But you won't need to. Almost any conversation contains *something* with which you can agree. Say so. "I agree with what you say about. . . ." Then add, "But I'm not too sure about some of the other parts. I'd have to think about that." This lets you be honest without being rude. It also helps the person feel that you are listening and struggling to understand his feelings. Most angry people don't need total agreement as much as they need to express their feelings to a listening ear. Smile, even when you disagree with him. Sometimes that's hard, especially if he is attacking something dear to you. But this gesture of acceptance helps redirect hostility into more logical channels.

Sometimes it helps to ask *why* he feels so strongly at certain points. Leftover anger is common in church people. A current matter reminds them of something similar that occurred long ago. Perhaps it happened in this church; perhaps in another congregation. The problem created an ecclesiastical catastrophe. Many people were hurt. Some left the church. The pastor resigned. Now they are fearful that the same thing could happen here and now.

"You really feel strongly about this. I wonder why?" Sometimes this honest inquiry releases an avalanche of old memories about a bad experience. Hearing that story may add volumes to your understanding of their anger. Now you know why the present situation raises so much concern.

Once that old story comes out in the open, you can sometimes say, "Do you really feel that our situation here will work out the same way that did?"

By that time, many people will say, "No, I guess this is not exactly the same thing. I suppose things will work out differently here. But we sure need to watch it. That kind of thing can really be a mess."

5. Ask them for suggestions about how this problem should be handled. Not too soon; wait until they have achieved total catharsis through the four steps above. Say something like, "What do you think ought to be done?" or "How do you feel we ought to handle this?" or "Do you have any ideas on that?"

Then listen. They may have a good idea that a less concerned person would never cook up. What they have so irascibly brought to your attention may be valid. And what if their solution is brilliant, needed, and simple? Don't risk missing good ideas just because they come from irritating people. Even if the idea is worthless, you might gain insights on future pressures they may place on the church. You thus win either way. If their solution sounds good, you can pass it on to a committee chairman or officer. If the idea stinks, you can plan defensive action to prevent a church dogfight.

On the other hand, they may say an amazing thing at this point: "Oh, I don't guess it really matters that much." Those words always mean that they didn't really want something changed; they just needed somebody to listen to them. Don't assume that every complainer wants something done. They don't. Sometimes they just feel neglected or sidelined. They need attention and don't know how else to get it.

A young pastor in his first church encountered a perpetual complaining machine. She stormed into his office every few weeks with a new problem that needed solving. Quickly and loudly unloading her angry feelings, she departed in a much better mood. He listened carefully and worked hard to fix what she wanted fixed. Two years of irritation later he realized that she didn't really want anything done about the problems. She wanted her pastor to listen. She needed some attention. By the time she got back home from blowing off steam, she could hardly remember what she had been upset about.

In football, linebacks are taught not to hit everything that comes through the line. Not the first thing; perhaps not even the second thing. They wait for the man carrying the little brown oblong ball. Such selectivity is necessary in dealing with angry church members. Some require careful attention and instant action. Others are just using you for an emotional pressure valve. So the best treatment is to listen carefully and not take them too seriously until you can decide whether they have the ball.

6. Tell them you appreciate their bringing it up. And you can do that sincerely. How much better for them to bring it up to you than to fifteen different people on the telephone! "How great a forest is set ablaze by a small fire!" James warns, speaking of the human tongue (James 3:5). Especially when angry people let their mouths run loose in a congregation. If they tell it to you, they may not tell it to so many others.

Some find it helpful to underline and memorize some of the key words above, like: *Sit, Listen, Agree, Why, Suggestions, Appreciate.* Angry people seldom give you time for advance thought preparation. It's easy to respond reflexively rather than thoughtfully. So sticking a formula in your head provides instant jujitsu with which to handle the unexpected. If you can keep your cool enough to use these six steps, you place the angry person at your mercy. You can beat him every time he plays this unexpected emotional checker game.

What causes most of the anger in church people? Certainly not logical, rational thinking. For 3,000 years, the world's best religious leaders have warned us against anger: "Anger in a wise man is never justified" (Buddhist saying from the *Jataka*). "When Mohammed was asked for advice, he said, 'Be not angry' " (The sayings of Mohammed as found in the Hadith). "A man of quick temper acts foolishly. . ." (Proverbs 14:17). "Let all bitterness and wrath and anger and clamor and slander be put away from you. . ." (Ephesians 4:31). With all that good advice, why do we blow our cool? Probably because we simply can't help it. The strong currents of emotional response continue to burst the best constructed dams of good intentions.

Some of these currents originate in the hidden springs of childhood patterns. People begin early to adopt one of three different reaction patterns in response to emotional pain. They handle stress either by running *away,* by running *toward,* or by running *against.* Some children, when hurt by parents, become silent and withdraw to their room. They reduce contact with the offending parties. They move *away.* Others, like the affectionate little girl who receives severe disciplining, withdraw into petulance for only a few moments. Then she runs back into the living room, jumps into her father's lap, and says, "Oh, Daddy, I really do love you." And he melts. She thus succeeds by moving *toward* the stress. Still another child finds that parents react best when he throws a temper tantrum. He wins by beating his head on the floor and screaming. He moves *against* stress.

How do these patterns work in the church? Those who typically respond by moving *away,* usually withdraw from active church life and are seldom heard from again. They become inactive. Those who tend to move *toward* may become briefly hostile. But later, they may increase efforts to serve the church. They may show up in the pastor's office with a thought-

44

ful gift. They may unexpectedly volunteer for a job. Sometimes they try to win with an artillery barrage of honeyed words, publicly bragging on the person who offended them. (Often, they are testing to see if the other person is still as angry as they themselves were.) Those who typically run *against* can be counted on in moments of church stress to go off like a roman candle. Anger is their knee jerk reflex to the stress of irritation and anxiety. As children, they generally had parents who weakened when their child got upset. So the anger worked. Parents either gave them what they wanted or became more affectionate, or both.

If anger worked well as a coping mechanism during childhood years, the individual naturally continues using it. It has always succeeded. Why change? Most church friends do not, however, respond to anger with affection as their former parents did. But the angry person doesn't know this. So he continues using his highly developed coping tool on people with whom it doesn't work. What can the church leader do to change this fruitless pattern? Very little. Full grown adults change their natural coping tendencies about as often as sparrows fly backwards. So understanding their pattern provides the best defense if you must work with them closely. Only then can you stop taking their anger quite so personally and learn to cope with their inadequate coping systems.

Don't, of course, infer that all anger in church stems from a childhood reflex. Even the most mature Christian occasionally suffers an attack of childish behavior. Sometimes she flips her top for no good reason. She didn't intend to, and feels sorry afterward. At other times, she hits the end of a long frustration rope and decides not to hang on. "Maybe this will get somebody's attention," she thinks. "Maybe then we can get something done around here." Sometimes she gets mad because she has indigestion; sometimes because she had a bad week at work. Sometimes she is mad at somebody at the office, so someone at church gets kicked with overflow anger. Why? They don't hold a position of authority from which to kick her back. Psychiatrists call this common behavior "displacement." Everybody does a little of it. Some do more than a little. But diagnosing the cause of anger is not that important anyway. Regardless of origin, the same general methods must be used in dealing with it effectively.

Many angry people are afraid of something—afraid of rejection, afraid of losing power, afraid of change. Ask yourself silently (never the angry person verbally), "What is this guy really afraid of?" Many of our deepest fears are too scary to admit; it's much easier to get mad than to look them in the eye.

Jonah grew furious when a shady plant wilted (Jonah 4:9). But underneath his anger lay the fear of losing prophetic face. God didn't deliver on Jonah's prediction of destruction for the city of Nineveh. How embarrassing for a prophet! (The heathen Ninevites did the unexpected—and from Jonah's point of view, the undesired. They repented and turned toward faith in the Jewish God.) Now the purity of the Hebrew church would be diluted with foreign blood. But Jonah could hardly express that fear to God. So he gets angry about a wilted plant instead.

Some anger originates with chronic unhappiness in private life. If a *woman* repeatedly expresses anger in church, suspect family problems. Is there continuing difficulty with father, mother, husband, children, or in-laws? Since the female ego structure requires success in these relationships, failure can cause severe loss of self-esteem. Fear and anger naturally result. So she unknowingly uses "displacement," venting her hostility on innocent bystanders in the church. While this safety valve helps her somewhat, it rarely helps the church people. They can't see the real source of her pain.

If a *man* is chronically hostile, overcritical, and overcontrolling, suspect vocational problems. Is he having trouble with the boss? Is he not being promoted fast enough? Does he have production problems? Is the business he owns going on the rocks financially? Are sales down? Since the male ego requires vocational success, apparent failure causes severe emotional pain. Some men therefore blow off their hostile feelings in the church setting. And where could they find a better place? Nobody in the church can fire them. They probably won't be asked to leave the membership, no matter how poor their behavior.

A manufacturing executive with a national firm stayed in middle management levels for ten years, stuck in the same small midwestern town. His brilliant mind was unfortunately housed in a dill pickle personality. Blessed with a high I.Q., his E.Q. (emotional quotient for relating to people) measured somewhere below moron. It was, of course, impossible for him to see this; harder still for his company to explain the reason for his lack of promotability. His frustration blew off on the church. He dominated all its meetings and actions. Having enough smarts to gain election to leadership positions, he found ample opportunity to control. His blowtorch temper made all board meetings an awesome spectacle. People stayed home in large bunches. In that small town, many people knew him well. So his caustic presence blocked the church from numerical growth. Few people wanted to sit in the same pew with his personality.

But then he ran for election to the local school board; surprisingly, he won. How that helped his self-esteem! Many demands were placed on his time. Many irate citizens called him daily for help with problems. He became important! And he simultaneously became a docile lamb in the church, easy to get along with. His need for church leadership roles ceased. He suggested that younger men take his place. After all, he was so busy. "And others need to learn leadership skills too," he said.

His earlier drive for vocational success evaporated, replaced by the community status success of serving on the school board. Freudian psychiatrists would call this "sublimation." He was now "sublimating" his powerful ego drives into constructive channels, rather than "displacing" his anger onto church people. But the story ends sadly. After election for one term on the school board, he lost a second term try, and thereby much self-esteem. (Elections are a brutal business; what people think of you is printed in the paper in the form of vote counts.) Within thirty days he reverted to his former role of resident pain in the neck. Once again he became the scourge of the minister, whom he succeeded in getting fired in another thirty days.

Handling the Perpetually Angry Member

What about the person who remains perpetually angry about the same thing? He expresses irritation about something, gets it off his chest. Then he does the same thing two weeks later, then again in a month. Everything is done about the problem which can be done. But he continues to gripe. How do you handle this person? You surely can't use the six point anger method mentioned earlier sixteen times on this same person, probably not even twice.

An automobile shop foreman taught his pastor a simple procedure for this. Another elder had been continually complaining about the same matter for weeks. Because of resentment over the unsolved problem, his church participation was declining. Other members were being influenced by his irritation.

One Saturday afternoon, the shop foreman, also an elder, went to visit Joe, the chronic complainer. "Joe, I've really been concerned about your attitude regarding the change in Sunday school starting time," he began.

Joe responded at length, as people always do when you call their attitude into question.

Then the foreman said, "You are a really important member of our church, Joe. The way you feel and what you say influences a lot of people."

And Joe responded, as people always do when you praise them.

"Joe, we need your help in this situation. Right now, there is no general agreement among our people about how to handle this. I think if we all keep working together in a positive way, we can eventually solve it. But we need the help of key people like yourself in order to do that."

Again, he gave Joe time to respond. And Joe did, in a positive way.

A crucial element in this procedure is having someone talk to Joe who knows him fairly well. An elder or key leader works best—never the preacher—in case Joe needs to blow off steam about him.

1. Go by and visit with Joe privately. Above all, do not visit in the presence of his spouse. Few men will ventilate real feelings or make themselves vulnerable in the presence of their spouses. Make the visit totally personal. Take him to coffee or lunch and say, "You know, Joe, I have really been concerned about your attitude regarding. . . . That has really bothered me." Don't talk to people about what they are doing wrong. Don't attack their behavior. If you do, they generally respond with anger and remind you that you are not so perfect either.

But if you tell me that my attitude is bad, I have a hard time defending myself against that. It must be observable or you wouldn't have seen it. If you have seen it, others probably have too. That likely turns me inward toward self-examination. So I tend to open up to you and talk out my feelings. Usually, I want to defend myself by letting you know the real cause

47

behind my attitude. Thus, catharsis begins, setting up a bond of positive feelings between the two of us.

"If your brother sins against you, go and tell him his fault, between you and him alone," says Jesus (Matthew 18:15). But very carefully. Begin your sentences with the pronoun "I." "I feel bad because. . . ." is a good example. The dangerous sentences begin with the pronoun "you." "You should not have. . . ." Such accusations build walls between people. They raise anger instead of reducing it. They threaten the person instead of helping him relax and express his feelings.

2. After Joe has talked his feelings out, say something like, "Well, I am concerned about you because I think a lot of you. You are a very important person in our church."

This encourages me to improve my attitude. After all, I certainly want my friends to maintain their positive feelings toward me. How people feel about me is far more important than any complaints I have.

3. Ask Joe's help. Few people can resist a direct request for help from someone who likes them.

This procedure for helping the chronic complainer doesn't always work. Don't use it frequently, and never on the same person twice. But when all else fails, it often resolves the seemingly unresolvable.

What about informing the pastor of problems and problem people? Many situations arise which he should know about. Isn't Sunday morning the logical time to do this? Perhaps after or before Sunday school. While this is great for minor matters, you couldn't pick worse timing for telling him about big problems. Leading a congregation in worship requires maximum concentration and emotional energy. At this apex of the week, every preacher wants to do his best. He strives for a clear mind in which the Spirit can move as he preaches. Dumping emotional garbage into the brain during the previous hour seldom aids him in achieving this goal. Do you really want to handicap your preacher? Right before church, tell him someone is working hard to get him fired. Then he can walk into the pulpit with that cheery news tugging at the frayed edges of his consciousness.

The second best time to clobber your pastor is right after the service. Preachers find themselves mentally and physically drained after preaching. Some experts say that delivering a sermon produces the physical equivalent of six hours of hard labor. Added to this, your pastor feels one of two ways after preaching. He may think, "Maybe it was a pretty good sermon. Nobody went to sleep and fell out of their pew into the floor. I felt that the Spirit really moved me, and people heard some words from God. Maybe I'm not a total failure at preaching after all." So a dedicated leader stays after church and lays some big bad news on him. What an excellent way to wilt a positive experience!

On the other hand, the pastor may feel like this: "What a bad day! I just never did get it together. I never got to the point on the way to the end of the sermon." He feels pretty low—wishes he had worked harder on his sermon—wonders if he has lost his touch. In that case, good friends can help him by handing him a bad problem to chew on. That will really give him something to feel lousy about.

Do you want to communicate about a really serious matter? Call him on the phone later this week. Stop by the office. Take him to lunch. But let him have this moment of glory—or go home to lick his wounded ego. This is no time to hear that Jim Jenson is quitting the church because somebody painted the men's rest room green.

Angry people often try to manipulate leaders into bypassing normal organizational procedures. Their definition of democracy goes like this: "If it's something someone else wants done, we vote on it. If it's something I want done, we do it immediately."

Some leaders develop memorized lines for instant recall at such moments: "That sounds like a good idea. Have you given that to the worship committee chairman?"

When the person replies in the negative, the leader can then say, "Why don't you talk to the chairman, Jim Jones. I'm sure he would be glad to discuss it with the committee. I can't predict how they would respond. But that's probably the best way to get a hearing on it." She has thereby replied positively, but avoided being used.

Suggesting referral of the matter to a committee has several advantages: It takes the fire off a particular individual, usually yourself. It allows time for a cooling off period. Later, this angry person can present his case much more rationally. But it also provides a concrete plan of action to help him feel he has accomplished *something*. His feelings will be heard.

At times, a leader may need to take direct action rather than referring someone to a committee. But we usually overestimate the frequency of this need. Some sage observed, "A man of great wrath will pay the penalty; for if you deliver him, you will only have to do it again" (Proverbs 19:19). Did you ever volunteer for go-between duty to keep an angry friend from making a fool of herself? If so, you probably got hooked. You never got finished acting as a go-between. And the first time you couldn't deliver exactly what he wanted, his double-barreled wrath turned toward you.

Only in rare situations should you say, "I'd be glad to pass this on to the board chairman if you'd like." The go-between usually ends up irritating people on both sides of the issue. When two sides throw rocks at each other, the person in the middle gets hit from both directions. Why? A person can never succeed at standing *exactly* in the middle. And from the viewpoint of each party, he appears to stand more toward the opposite side. The two quarreling parties eventually agree on at least one thing: They don't like the mediator. Many leaders collect severe emotional concussions while learning this simple lesson.

In a few conversations, you can invite the angry person to serve on the committee in charge of his concern. Nothing leavens the loaf of understanding like direct responsibility for the problem. He gets to hear six other opinions about how to handle it. And sometimes he discovers logical reasons why his pet project just won't fly.

One church suddenly accrued several angry members because of homosexuality resolutions at a national assembly. So the board chairman put these angry persons on a special committee to draft a protest letter to various national leaders. Designing the letter allowed time to vent angry feelings. Each of the committee members then felt, "We have taken action; we have done something about this problem." Most situations can't be handled this way, but some can. Nothing reduces irritation like taking concrete action to deal with the offending problem.

What about the abrasive person who takes and keeps control of everything in the church? One small town church is dominated by the only banker in town. Since every member in that little Kansas community must eventually borrow money at his bank, they dare not disagree with him. Those who do will hear more than harsh words; he refuses their next loan request.

Such situations are best dealt with through spiritual means. Solutions must be built on close-knit emotional and spiritual fellowship between the minister and key leaders. If this cannot be achieved, leaders generally end up defending the problem member and uniting against the pastor. They will find it more convenient to move the pastor to another church than to battle a long-term community figure. Chapter one illustrates the best possible means for arresting this typical syndrome with spiritual intervention. If the dominating person is part of the key leadership group, chances for a good resolution are increased. If the individual is outside the key leadership group and exerts underground control through money or business pressure, the problem is less capable of resolution.

A dominating matriarch controlled one congregation for fifty years. Her mother before her had done the same. Since 1888, the average tenure of a pastor has been twenty-one months. Of the last four ministers, two committed suicide and the other two left the ministry. Most members felt helpless to change things. Others felt that they must love her instead of dealing with her behavior. (A remarkable view, since fifty years of this approach has not helped.) Some members were blood relatives. They humored her in order to prevent conflict in the church (though conflict is omnipresent).

In a small community where many business people are financially and socially interdependent, such problems are difficult to resolve. At the bottom line, the elders or key officer group must decide what they value most. Is church democracy the highest value? Or do they value avoiding conflict with a particular individual?

Jesus prescribed methods for resolving such matters in Matthew 18:15-18. "If your brother sins against you, go and tell him his fault, between you and him alone. If he listens to you, you have gained your brother. But if he does not listen, take one or two others along with you, that every word may be confirmed by the evidence of two or three witnesses. If he refuses to listen to them, tell it to the church; and if he refuses to listen even to the church, let him be to you as a Gentile and a tax collector.

Truly, I say to you, whatever you bind on earth shall be bound in heaven, and whatever you loose on earth shall be loosed in heaven."

Paul says that leaders have a right to judge people in the church. "For what have I to do with judging outsiders? Is it not those inside the church whom you are to judge? God judges those outside" (1 Cor. 5:12-13).

But most leaders find it difficult to take these suggestions seriously. They dissect the scriptures and use only those they find tasteful. Texts on love are taken literally. Texts on discipline are identified as rising from infantile stages of development in the early church—thus not usable. But both types still have contemporary application. The most loving thing we can do for some people is force them to lay down their burden of running everything.

Many people misunderstand Jesus when he says, "Blessed are the peacemakers, for they shall be called sons of God" (Matthew 5:9). They think he means, "Blessed are the *peace lovers*." Almost anyone would qualify as a peace lover. But becoming a peacemaker takes more than pleasant thoughts. It means accepting leadership responsibility, the willingness to face conflict, and sometimes daring to run risks.

Leaders in one church took unexpected action against a ruling elderess. Going to her as a group, they told her kindly but firmly that they would not continue to tolerate her behavior. Her well-meaning control was hindering the church. They didn't threaten her with expulsion, but they did place her on a one year probation. An exceptional case, and very few should be handled this way. But they were taking Matthew's chapter eighteen seriously. They were valuing their Lord's work more than personal fear of conflict. And their method worked.

"Appoint only veteran members to the high mortality rate job of property chairman."

5 Alice Doesn't Live Here Anymore

The Inactive Member

Joe Jamieson felt a pull of nostalgia as the familiar steet unwound before his bumper. Up to Third Avenue, then right to Hillside, the Chevy rolled to a stop in front of towering old First Church. That building where he had worked so hard as a pastor still seemed like home; ten years had not dulled his love for its old bricks. Summer vacation had been restful, and topping it off with a swing through Clinesville made a perfect ending. This familiar tree-lined street put him in touch with the best side of himself.

Later, he sat drinking coffee with the present pastor in the parsonage kitchen. Exchanging bits of information about the church, Joe was curious to know who was still here after ten years. Only a few. In this transient oil field community, most members moved sooner than their pastor. Companies whisked them off to Houston or Tripoli with unexpected regularity. What a strange new world. Just imagine, the pastor staying around longer than most members. How the world had changed! But when Joe mentioned the name of one couple who he knew still lived in town, the new pastor looked blank. "Oh, I've seen their name on the roll," he said. "But I guess they're deadwood. I've never seen them in church."

Joe was astonished. The husband had served as board chairman twelve years ago. He had been a good friend and a loyal supporter, a Christian of unblemished dedication. "What happened?" he asked. "Why did they drop out?"

"I don't know. I guess it must have happened before my time. Ken Triplett served as pastor for five years between the time that you and I served. Maybe it happened while he was here."

Probable Causes for Inactivity

Every leader knows a similar story. But what causes this? Why do active members fall away? What can be done about it? More answers are now available for these questions than ever before in history. The pioneering work of John S. Savage as reported in *The Apathetic and Bored Church Member* (Lead Consultants, P.O. Box 311, Pittsford, New York 14534, 1976) has begun to do for our understanding of the inactive member what Elisabeth Kubler-Ross did to help us understand the stages of the terminally ill. Though the following analysis differs from his at many points, anyone working in this field must stand on the shoulders of his insights.

Movement toward inactivity *begins* when a specific upsetting event throws a member off balance emotionally. This experience produces such inner anxiety that they feel uncomfortable in church. The top four upsetting events are listed below in order of greatest frequency. These account for most dropouts; causes four through eight account for a few.

1. Conflict with the pastor (or traumatic loss of the affectionate bond). Rather than a generalized irritation, this conflict always begins with a specific event. One pastor just beginning in a new parish visited an adult Sunday school class. During the discussion, the question arose of whether you must regularly attend church in order to qualify for the label of Christian. The young pastor, fresh from theological training, laid out the biblical reasons why real Christians always participate in church life. The discussion heated mildly, but no more than most class conversations. He promptly forgot the event.

Unknown to him, one of the couples had only recently begun attending church. They did not verbalize any opinion at all during the class session, but the following week they vanished from church attendance. All attempts failed to find out why. Finally, nine months later, they told someone the truth. The new minister's attitude bothered them. "He calls people unchristian if they don't attend church." They felt he was judging too harshly. They didn't wish to attend a church where the pastor held that view.

Sometimes, however, the conflict erupts in a manner obvious to all observers. The pastor dragged himself to a wedding rehearsal. Weary from a long week of night calls and difficult days, he felt exhausted. The mother of the bride immediately made it clear that she would direct this rehearsal. After all, this was *her daughter's* wedding! The minister disagreed. He told her firmly who was going to tell who what to do and where to stand. Unfortunately, he told her so directly that she got more than the

54

message; she got angry. After the wedding, she was never again seen at church. For years afterward she told her friends how the pastor had "cussed her out" for attending her daughter's wedding rehearsal.

More frequently, the conflict with the pastor remains unknown to him. Finally, months or years later, he finds out. In one church, the board appointed a committee to decorate the new parlor. At the committee's first meeting one woman suggested blue for the color of the drapes. The pastor carefully and quietly conjectured, "I wonder how they would look in green?" The discussion passed on. Several people suggested other colors. Ultimately, neither green nor blue was chosen.

But the woman who had made the blue suggestion went away from the meeting feeling, "the pastor doesn't like me." The more she thought about it, the more angry she became. "He really must think I'm a dummy." And the more she thought about it, the more she realized how rude he had been. The following week they met at a wedding reception. As they drank coffee and chatted, she felt he was ill at ease. *He really didn't want to talk with me,* she thought. *At the first opportunity, he excused himself and walked over to visit with someone else.*

The following Sunday morning sermon pointed at Christians who lacked a cooperative spirit. The conclusion called for love and understanding between church people. Now she was sure. "He directed that at me. What nerve! Preaching a whole sermon to get even with one person!" The following week she was conveniently ill. The second Sunday she visited relatives in Detroit. The third week she attended another church with a friend. When asked why she moved her membership four months later, she replied, "I just didn't feel comfortable there anymore. Since Rev. Smith came, the church has changed. It isn't warm and friendly like it used to be."

Such neurotic behavior accounts for many church dropouts. If tested with an MMPI (Minnesota Multiphasic Personality Inventory), this lady would have shown an elevated paranoia scale. Her pattern throughout life had been to withdraw from people with whom she felt differences of opinion. Dropping out of church was one more example on a long list resulting from that temperament trait.

Churches and ministers unknowingly serve as parent figures for us in grownup years. Thus, our relationships with them often play back emotional tapes stored in our minds since childhood. Rejection or "imagined rejection" by parents produces great hurt in some people during youthful years. So when a similar thing seems to happen in adult years, terrible pain results. Consequently, such persons naturally withdraw from the perceived pain source.

The reaction of members who carry this basic response pattern is hard to defend against. If they openly exploded, their problem could be more easily handled. But dealing with their hidden anxiety is like trying to put out a fire without knowing its location.

2. Conflict with another church member. Bill Witherspoon and George Thomas served on the building committee together. A building supply salesman, Bill possessed some knowledge of construction processes. But as chairman of the committee, George felt the heaviest burden of responsibility. *The congregation will blame me if anything goes wrong,* he thought.

One day after the building began taking skeleton shape, Bill stopped by to check the progress. Seeing a door of the wrong size in the baptistry framing, he called it to the contractor's attention. After consulting the blueprints, the builder found that Bill was right. The offending door really belonged in a nearby janitor's closet. The profuse thanks made Bill feel good. His intervention had prevented an expensive replacement process.

Later that day George, the building committee chairman, came by. The contractor reported the door goof to him and expressed appreciation for Bill's alert eye. But George went home angry. "That Bill always butts in where he doesn't belong. Only a week ago the building committee had agreed that the contractor must have only one boss—George. Everyone had promised to funnel all complaints through him." George was still seething when he saw Bill the next Sunday. As they drank coffee before Sunday school, he thought about how to bring it up. But somehow the proper words never came to mind. After all, Bill had been right about the door. But the principle of the whole thing made him mad.

The following week George laid his resignation on the pastor's desk. It covered almost everything. He resigned as building committee chairman, deacon, and property chairman. His reasons? Personal. George didn't withdraw his membership. But he may as well have. His cabin on the lake, grandchildren, and woodworking hobby now take up all his time. He and Sarah rarely appear in church anymore.

3. Conflict with a family member. Kip and Joanne had been church active since early marriage. Before the first baby, they led the high school youth program. Time passed. Joanne arrived at age thirty-six. Phase one of her mid-life crisis began when her mirror reported fading beauty. "Youth is almost gone," she thought. Needing reassurance about her attractiveness, she found it readily available from her office supervisor. The infatuation became an affair, which became a family explosion when a friend told Kip.

Not wanting the marriage to shatter, both worked hard at reconciliation. During this time, Kip wondered if they were putting too much time into church activities. Perhaps they should invest more in each other. Besides, he was embarrassed. Several church friends knew about his wife's indiscretions. His responsibility level as a vestryman diminished along with their worship attendance.

Joanne had always found intellectual pursuits more fascinating than church work. Hoping that a change would help her depression, she enrolled in an evening course at the junior college. Learning that Kip had discussed their problem with the pastor hadn't helped. Excuses for skipping church came easy now. The added load of college work made it hard to get up in time for Sunday school. She had always been a late sleeper anyway.

Kip and Joanne may never resume church activity. If they do, it will likely be in some other congregation. They don't really feel at home in their church anymore. So many new faces inhabit the pews now. They feel out of touch and out of place.

4. The overworked, burned out syndrome—too much, too soon. Carol Stinson was happy in her new church home. Fitting into a new community came easier because of friends she found there. A pleasing smile and quick wit coupled with an outgoing personality propelled her into several leadership roles. Within two years she had accumulated an impressive list of titles: junior high Sunday school teacher, evangelism calling committee, volunteer helper at the church office. When Carol's husband wanted to reach her, he usually telephoned the church. He was more likely to find her there than at home.

Then, before anyone realized it, Carol reached her saturation point. The joy drained out of her superactivity. Constant tiredness cancelled out the ego charge she got from leadership. Then came the "elder brother feeling" so common among overproductive church leaders: "It irritates me to death when people don't carry out their responsibilities. I get *my* work done. Why can't they? If you want anything done around here, you have to do it yourself."

On top of this came a mid-life year when she felt physically exhausted all the time. During this period, her church attitude soured. "Poor little me" thoughts replaced "isn't this fun" emotions. "Can't anyone but me do anything at that church? Why do they always call *me*?" Even for wedding receptions, someone always asked her to help supervise. After all, she knew where everything was.

Self-pity slowly changed to anger. At first it was anger at other people for using her. "They are taking advantage of me." Then it was anger at herself for letting them. The anger finally exploded into action. She would stop letting people use her. She had nothing against the pastor, liked him very much. But she was through acting like a flesh and blood doormat. It took an hour to write out resignations from all her jobs. But her resolve held firm. After dropping part of them in the mail and delivering the others, she felt much better. "I'm taking charge of my own life. I'll certainly never again let myself get that tangled up in anything."

Nobody could understand why she resigned. She had always seemed so eager to help. And she had *volunteered* for much of her work load. Puzzled, nobody pressed the issue. "She must be mad at someone in the women's group," some thought. "She'll get over it."

But Carol's resignations didn't make her feel as happy as she had hoped. Now she felt guilty. She had left so many friends holding so many bags full of work. Then too, every time she attended something, she saw what a bumbling job her replacements were doing. "How irritating to see everything going wrong. And everybody is probably blaming me for not continuing my responsibility."

Carol was trapped in a double bind. She couldn't keep up her wonder-woman act, either physically or emotionally. But she couldn't stand to watch her replacements foul up. So she took the only way out—the back door. Staying home on Sunday, she soon found a good religious program on television. A California production mixing show business with optimism, it left her feeling happy and positive. *One thing about a TV service,* she thought, *you don't have to direct the choir, wash the communion cups, and cut the bulletin stencils.*

As the year passed, Carol wondered why she had been so active in church anyway. She certainly wouldn't make that silly mistake again. All church callers were greeted with courtesy. Genuinely glad to visit with them, she sincerely urged them to come back. She held no antagonisms toward them. Some were still good friends and would remain so. She was just a lot happier attending a television set than a building.

Another form of this same reaction pattern goes like this: A carpenter joins a church at middle life. A small congregation, they appoint him property chairman the following year. He feels honored and accepts with enthusiasm, expecting plenty of help from other members. But he can't understand why so few show up to help with the spring cleanup day. Do they not like him personally? That summer he paints the building by himself during evenings and vacation time. By now he has concluded that other members just don't care about their properties. This changes to self-pity, then to feeling used, then to resignation and dropping out. Like a meteor, he did an amazing amount of work during that year. But also meteorlike, he falls to earth permanently. No more church for him. He has learned his lesson about church people. "They are all a bunch of hypocrites."

A good rule: Appoint only veteran members to the high mortality rate job of property and grounds chairman. Only a strong "upper" personality can handle this "downer" job. The work consists mostly of thankless tasks rarely seen and appreciated by other members. So he gets little praise for his efforts. Nor does he find much fellowship in the work. Most of it is done when the other members are absent from the building. He often hears critical remarks about his department. "The kindergarten class room is so dirty!" "Nobody ever fixed that air conditioner after I reported it two times!"

5. Moral problem. A minister moved from seminary graduation to his first full-time church. Beginning to get acquainted, he heard reports on the church's most recent internal disaster. A key leader, real estate broker by profession, had resigned from all duties three months before. The young preacher could never quite get at the truth of what had alienated the man. His parishioners in this small Texas town told slightly differing stories, but most of them revolved around a liquor store property the broker had taken against a bad debt. The previous pastor, adamantly opposed to alcohol, had immediately preached a sermon on the subject. Four weeks elapsed and the broker still hadn't sold the place. So the preacher pulled the trigger on his second homiletical shotgun barrel.

This time, he called the man by name from the pulpit. In the ill winds that ensued, various leaders took sides. The broker didn't sell; he dropped out.

The new pastor tried everything in the effort to get him back. He drank three barrels of coffee with the man over a five-year period. He urged him to assume particular responsibilities in the church. He told him how much the church needed him. He eventually could say, "Many of the people you had the trouble with have now moved out of town." But the man showed up at Sunday worship about three times a year, never more.

Seven years later, the pastor felt like a fool when he learned the real truth. Everyone in town had known it but him. The broker was sleeping with his secretary. Church leaders had known this for years, but felt helpless to confront him. The liquor store incident finally gave them opportunity to deal with him without mentioning his sexual escapades.

The broker never admitted to himself that anyone knew the real truth. But every time he attended church, he suffered moral anxiety. Sitting in an atmosphere where conscience confronted moral behavior always brought his inner conflict to the surface. He couldn't tolerate more than three doses of that each year.

6. Various forms of life change. An upward job mobility may thrust people into a different social climate which includes weekend trips and events. Church becomes more inconvenient and less attractive. Such changes face the individual into *conscious* decisions about church, perhaps for the first time. Maybe he grew up attending church as naturally as brushing his teeth. When he married, that pattern continued. But now, time priorities must be set intentionally, not accidentally. So church activity fades into number three position. *It just doesn't seem that important,* he thinks. *My job simply has to come first.*

Children growing up and leaving home bring another dramatic life change. "We used to go all the time," a previously active couple says to callers for the next twenty years. "But now that the children are grown, we just don't go much. You know how it is." This type of person views the church as an institution like a high school, designed to provide them a service. So when their service need ends, they stop participation. They never seem to perceive that churches meet our need for self-giving as well as self-getting. (Or perhaps they simply aren't interested in self-giving?)

In another pattern, the man receives a demotion, suffers a business failure, or loses his job. His sudden drop in self-esteem stock then devalues his church ties at the very time he needs them most. "Oh, what's the use," he thinks about his vocational future. And this depressive fog spreads quite naturally to his church relationships. So he withdraws into himself or diverts his attention to something radically different, like fishing. He usually remains unaware that psychological pain has poisoned the springs of his Christian faith. *I just don't get much out of church anymore,* he thinks.

If his job stress produces *severe* depression, a compound fracture can result. He often creates an emotionally upsetting event by getting angry at someone in the church. And since getting angry usually makes depressed people feel less depressed, no logic will encourage him to let go of it. Why let go of something which protects you from inner pain? In this situation, all successful procedures are blocked. Only when the depression lifts will he possibly return. But as time passes, other habits replace church habits so that returning seems unnatural.

Death of a parent or relative sometimes precipitates another variety of this pattern. Losing someone suddenly or traumatically causes some theologically shallow personalities to respond, "I don't know whether I believe in God anymore. If God is real, why did he let my mother die of cancer?" This reaction is not just psychological, but theological as well. The anger that serves as a shield against depression is directed toward God instead of another person. So if the individual returns to church, he must drop his anger against God—something he is subconsciously unwilling to do because it may cause him to get depressed again.

A leader who suspects this problem should loan the person a copy of Leslie Weatherhead's little book, *The Will of God*. For parishioners who don't like to read, cassette tapes of this excellent book are now available. Such material often allows the grieving person to find a third alternative—acceptance of the loss. Rather than flip-flopping between painful depression and suppressed anger at God, they can begin accepting reality. Unfortunately, pastors frequently fail to learn of this dilemma. People fear to bring it up with him. How do you diplomatically tell your minister that you have become an atheist? It is easier to find some other excuse for not attending church.

Divorce brings another radical life change which easily leads to church inactivity. Divorced people feel guilty because their marriage failed. Ill at ease with themselves, they now feel uncomfortable worshiping with old friends. Each service forces them to a painful comparison between past and present life. Their uneasiness increases because church friends don't know what to say. *If I sympathize, I may appear to be taking sides,* they think. *I don't wish to do that since both partners are my friends. But if I say nothing, I may also seem to be taking sides.* Caught in this impossible bind, friends often retreat socially. Verbal contacts reduce to a courteous minimum until the divorce storm has clearly passed.

The divorced person often misperceives such a defensive reaction and feels shunned. "People are blaming me for the divorce," they think. "And how awkward singlehood feels after all these years! All the social events are so couple oriented." The single woman feels especially uncertain about whether wives really want her there. And how should she behave if she goes? "Aren't married women threatened by a free-floating female?" she asks herself. "Will they misinterpret my friendliness as an amorous intent toward their husbands?"

The divorcée usually misguesses when she thinks married women feel jealous. But not always! Every church contains a number of "close to the rocks" marriages. Such wives seldom enjoy attractive females exchanging friendly conversation with their husbands at fellowship dinners.

But how do you discuss these fears with a church visitor? With great difficulty. Why not pretend that you are too busy? Or you can say, "I'm involved in so many other things right now. And of course I have to clean house over the weekends."

7. *Personal financial problems.* Among the top three killers of marriages in the United States, conflict over finances ranks second. Poor cash flow also accounts for a few church membership divorces. When money trouble hits a family, the husband feels like a failure: "I'm not man enough to support my family." The wife suffers lowered self-esteem in her household management role: "I'm just not smart enough to keep the slippery ends of the budget together." Unconsciously, both begin to handle their blues by picking each other apart. Quarreling patterns escalate. This hypercritical attitude soon spreads to other parts of their life, like church. Worship service becomes painful rather than inspiring. The passing offering plate says to them, "You are failing here too!" So they gradually fade away from worship, often giving callers some phony reason for reduced attendance.

8. *The failing Band-Aid syndrome.* Unchurched couples with a falling apart marriage may suddenly start attending church. The following Sunday, they join. Two weeks later they stop attending and get a divorce. Neither ever shows for church again.

A person under psychiatric care (usually schizophrenic or depressive) may suddenly start attending church. Trying to fight their illness with spiritual power, they volunteer for youth work or other programs. After three Sundays of religion makes them feel no better, they drop away.

The Stages to Inactivity

Like those reacting to deep grief, people move through definite stages on their trip to inactivity. The characteristic flight pattern from active to inactive membership status goes like this:

1. *Most people begin by verbalizing their irritation with something or someone.*

2. *If nobody seems to listen, they get louder.* Some get louder verbally. Others get louder quietly, by passive-aggressive methods. Turning irresponsible in committee work, they act generally irritated and cynical.

3. *If still no one listens, they get angry.* Sometimes that anger lashes out against the source of their anxiety. More often, complaints strike at sideline issues. In that way, anger vents in a nonthreatening way. They don't have to admit what or who they are really mad at. So nobody gets the chance to tell them how silly it is.

4. *Next, they drop out of worship attendance.* "I'll punish them by my absence," describes the inner thought pattern. "I'll show them. I don't *have* to go to church there."

5. *They expect someone to notice their absence and come to find out why.* If no one comes to inquire about their absent condition, they act out their

anger. As well as staying out of worship, they stop committee work and other responsibilities.

6. In a final angry act, they shut off financial support. Several months may have passed since they last attended. But monthly stewardship checks keep on arriving at the church by mail. Done partly as an attention-getting protest, this also allows them to feel self-righteous. "I never attend, but I still give my money. I'm one of the largest contributors down there." But self-defense also motivates this behavior. Stopping stewardship would have furnished church leaders with a rational reason *for getting angry with them.* They don't want that to happen. They still hope someone will come and help them to feel good about getting active again.

But what about someone who stops giving money immediately, before he quits attending? This apparent exception isn't. Appearing mostly in smaller churches, this pocketbook power player intends to force submission. Or, he plans to force pastoral relocation to some comfortably distant parish. But note that this type of person has no intention of withdrawing from his source of emotional upset. He plans to exert power and control over it.

7. The member now feels helpless. He silently blames other church people for his misery and thinks, *Nobody cares. No one is going to come and help me with my problem.* He feels that the matter is now out of his hands; he can do nothing to resolve his alienation.

Another kind of person may internalize his anger at this stage. He feels guilty and unworthy of church participation. Sometimes genuine, this guilty feeling more often protects him from admitting his own anger. As long as he feels guilty and depressed, he doesn't have to admit to himself how mad he is.

8. He ceases to care about church relationships. At this stage, he has so redirected habit patterns and life energies that reactivation becomes difficult. Then too, returning would force internal admission of his earlier anger. Who likes to admit that he got mad or made a silly mistake? Not many. So his self-protection system locks him out of retracing his steps and repairing the relationship.

Reactivating Inactives

How to call on the inactive member? Many dedicated leaders raise a prior question, "Why call at all? Why should we bother with him?"

For the purely selfish reason of getting him to work in and support the church. And certainly for humanistic reasons—because we care about him. But beyond this, for theological reasons.

". . .am I my brother's keeper?" asks Cain (Genesis 4:9).

"Yes," answers the New Testament. "For if you love those who love you, what reward have you? Do not even the tax collectors do the same?

And if you salute only your brethren, what more are you doing than others? Do not even the Gentiles do the same? You, therefore, must be perfect, as your heavenly Father is perfect" (Matthew 5:46-48).

Those who take the controls of an airplane without some pilot instruction seldom fly well. They usually damage the plane, the runway, or themselves. Similar results usually come to those using guesswork procedures to call on inactives. Here, as in dealing with angry people, certain techniques work; others don't. They may even drive people into confirmed inactivity rather than encouraging them to return. Charlie Brown, the child cartoon character created by Charlie Schultz, always wonders why he loses so many softball games. After all, he is so sincere! Inactive member calling numbers among those many life experiences where sincerity alone doesn't win games. We must know what to do and say, and especially what not to say. The following points can arm us with those insights.

1. Understand that hostility is not the basic emotion behind withdrawal from activity. Inactives move through several stages of intense pain more similar to grief reactions than to anger states. "I wish someone would help me resolve my terrible sense of alienation," they are saying. "I have lost an important relationship with my church and my pastor. That bothers me terribly." Understanding this unspoken pain helps the caller develop a compassionate attitude more likely to produce success.

2. Call during the first six weeks after worship attendance stops. Success ratios reduce radically after this time period. People arrive at the "I don't give a damn anymore" terminal on different time schedules. But once there, almost nothing can start them back the other direction. Up until six weeks passes, they may not be there yet; after that they likely will. This makes some systematic process for obtaining names of those who attend Sunday worship of crucial importance. Without this, and without specific leaders assuming responsibility for certain families, late timing makes most calls worthless.

Leaders usually delay calls beyond the "point of no return" for three reasons: Firstly, they don't understand the progressive stages. Secondly, they don't know how to make the call. Thirdly, ". . .the spirit indeed is willing, but the flesh is weak" (Matthew 26:41).

3. Make the call with only one aim in mind–listening to their story. The natural inclinations of church callers run more toward *telling* than listening. But in this instance a telling stance always proves disastrous. Nothing you can tell them will reactivate them. On the contrary, it will probably anger them. Your ear, not your mouth, is the essential tool for this kind of call.

Some callers simply cannot restrain themselves from "telling people a thing or two." Leaders should bodily restrain such persons from making inactive member calls. "Judge not, that you be not judged. For with the judgment you pronounce you will be judged, and the measure you give will be the measure you get'' (Matthew 7:1-2). Especially on inactive member calls. "Hatred is not diminished by hatred at any time. Hatred is diminished by love—this is the eternal law" (Buddhist saying from the *Dhammapada, 5*).

4. Never make defensive statements about yourself, the church, God, other members, or the pastor. Just listen, try to understand, and communicate your understanding. "See that none of you repays evil for evil. . ." Paul says (1 Thessalonians 5:15). Double that advice for inactive member calls. You can't win a smiting contest in this stadium. So leave your well-reasoned arguments at home. Take only two listening ears that bear all without rebuttal.

5. Emphasize responsive listening techniques. Salt conversation heavily with sentences that begin with, "You feel like. . . ." Add to those three words your understanding of what they just finished expressing. Imagine yourself as a human mirror, constantly reflecting the words and feelings of your conversational partner. This responsive approach helps people move past defensive irritation to deeper matters. Consequently, they start feeling understood, warm toward the caller, and begin shaking loose from previous hostility.

6. Possible conversational steps. First, visit for about five minutes on general topics. Then say, "I've been concerned about you, Larry. I haven't seen you in church for some time. Since I know you are a person of real integrity, I'm sure there must be some good reason why you stopped attending."

This always brings some type of response. Keep your mouth firmly shut and give them plenty of time. After a stumbling beginning, they will take one of two directions. Some will begin the story they have been wanting to tell someone. Others will offer a superficial excuse to hide their real feelings. Either way, this conversational opener allows you to pursue their concerns.

What if they seem unwilling to talk? Try saying something like, "You may feel that you'd rather not share your painful feelings with me. But in some ways you already have. You have said with your absence what you have not said verbally. I would very much like to know the cause of your feelings. I know you are a good person, and I'm sure there must be a good reason."

If they stick with an evasive answer, another effective approach goes like this: "I feel like someone in our church must have made a real blunder. Perhaps it was me. Won't you please tell me what it was, Larry?"

If Larry persists in using his unreal excuse, say, "In addition to that, isn't there some other reason? Isn't there something else in the back of your mind?" Effective salesmen have used this old "in addition to that" phrase for years to find out the real reason why customers stopped buying their product. It works equally well in the church.

Some like to add the following phrases to that magic mind zipper: "If there is something else, and we can't clear it up, you'll at least feel better for having given us the chance. On the other hand, if we are somehow able to clear it up, you'll feel better for giving us the chance to correct the wrong. Isn't that right, Larry?''

Less than 5 percent can resist this honest expression of concern. But what if they still withhold their story? Perhaps they are fearful of conflict, or afraid of becoming angry and upset by expressing their hurt. If so, move to your last ditch approach. ''I know you may not want to tell me the reason why you stopped coming, but I'd really like to know. Of course, if you'd rather not discuss it, that's OK.'' Then shut up and wait for the silence to start them talking.

This permission to withhold the story generally has the opposite effect. They immediately want to tell you about it. Many psychiatrists use this kind of statement to begin their first session with fearful patients. ''I know there are things that you may wish to withhold from me because you don't know me very well. If that is the case, I certainly understand. Please feel free to hold back anything you don't wish to tell me until we get better acquainted.''

Such statements usually free up the patient to express deeper feelings sooner. He feels an overwhelming compulsion to tell all to someone who tells him he doesn't have to. The psychiatrist has removed himself from the parental authority role. He has intentionally placed himself at the mercy of the patient. In so doing, he gives the patient the self-confidence and ease that comes from complete control of the situation.

When they have decided to tell you, listen attentively to their story. Don't fill pregnant pauses with anecdotes and remarks. They may find their story difficult to tell. So don't be surprised if great emotion comes out with it. When a tearful person breaks down and apologizes for crying, say, ''That's OK. There is nothing wrong with crying. Sometimes it helps a lot. I understand how you feel, so don't worry about a few tears.''

When you are absolutely certain they have finished their story, say, ''What can we do to make you feel more comfortable about coming back to church?''

Again, listen carefully. They probably don't want you to do anything. They usually start listing things they themselves ought to do. They now tell you faults you felt the urge to confront them with at the beginning. Why does this happen? You cared enough to come and listen to them without judging them. That makes them feel warm toward you. They want to repay your concern by doing the right thing.

Finally, complete the call by saying, ''I really appreciate your willingness to be honest about your feelings.'' And you should. Most people have heard about the ''priesthood of all believers.'' But you have lived it out. You have heard their confession of anger, guilt, hurt, and loss. You have listened to their resolve to do better. What a sacred relationship! What a sacred communication! Few church members ever have this privilege.

65

Long-Term Inactives

What about the member inactive for several years? These persons are difficult to reach with any approach. Apathy has replaced their desire for reconciliation. In fact, certain personality types now get more emotional charge out of staying away from church than from going. (As they enjoyed resisting parental authority during adolescence, they now enjoy resisting the authority of the church.)

One congregation sets aside one month each year for the elders to call on all the inactives. During that month—August—the minister also calls on them. Since people expect a lecture, callers surprise them by not giving them one. "How are you? How are things going?" describes the conversational approach. This leaves callees nothing to resist and react against. How can you react against active love and interest?

Not many per year reactivate from this "August method," perhaps one or two. But attitudes and circumstances can change in twelve months. So in case their minds are fertile for reentry into the church at this life stage, the opportunity is offered. Churches which show enough concern for inactives to call on them once each year accomplish three things: Firstly, nobody can say, "They never call on me except when they are asking for money." Secondly, active love and acceptance may influence them. Thirdly, ministers and leaders don't feel guilty the rest of the year because "we aren't doing anything to reach these people."

Why do persons *not* quit the church?

Looking at the issue from its positive side, why do most persons stay active while others in the same congregation drop away? Childhood training and psychological makeup exert great influence. But most active people share the following qualities:

1. They have an affectionate bond with the minister. Each member feels entitled to this, and it generally begins prior to joining the church.

2. They have a warm relationship with two or more families in the church. In addition to the pastor, they can confide in and discuss things with these friends.

3. They have a supportive relationship with some small group in the church. This could be a study group, prayer group, softball team, or service activity. Whatever its focus, this group provides a basic necessity of life—the chance to relate to others in a personal way.

4. They have some type of responsibility in the church. This task enhances their self-esteem. They feel appreciated, respected, and needed.

5. They have a sense of loyalty and devotion to God. This spiritual view of life nourishes their feeling of responsibility toward the church. But if the first four factors are missing, this alone will not keep them active.

6 Overcoming Evangelphobia

The Evangelism Call

The average male in the United States has 2.21 phobias. The average female has 3.55 phobias. (Phobia: an extreme and unnecessary fear of something—like fear of being trapped in an elevator.) The average church member of both sexes has one additional phobia—evangelphobia—fear of making evangelism calls. Jesus said, "Go therefore and make disciples of all nations. . ." (Matthew 28:19). Most of his modern followers are afraid to go across the street. They would rather make three hospital calls than one visit to a potential new member.

One woman describes her mental block about evangelism work like this: "I just can't do that sort of thing. I'll teach a class or work in the kitchen, anything else. But calling just isn't my thing. Even if I did go calling, I wouldn't know what to say. Even if I did say the right thing, it probably wouldn't do any good anyway."

But these negative feelings about evangelistic calling are only one pole of a strange paradox. A recent study shows that lay people in seventeen denominations think evangelism is crucially important. In fact, they feel it is more important than their pastors do.[1]

The lay people are obviously right. The future of *every* congregation depends on replacing people who continually move away. And studies of rapidly growing churches across the United States show that they have at least one thing in common—a high volume of face-to-face contacts between members and nonmembers. Verbal procedures used in the call differ radically among these congregations. But all growing churches work hard at influencing other people toward their church. And they all use some kind of eyeball-to-eyeball approach.

What produces this ironic paradox? We feel that evangelism calling should be done. Statistics show that it *must* be done. So why don't we want to do it? Partly from lack of personal motivation. (Like some other church chores, we want it done but we don't *personally* want to do it.) But mostly from lack of know-how. Could-be callers lack the self-confidence that comes with knowing how to do a job well. So they stay home.

How can this dilemma be corrected? The following outline can help. This isn't the *only* way to make a call. Some conservative Christians who like to use a more hard-sell approach will judge it superficial. Extreme liberals who have never made such a call may see it as *too direct*. But the method has one significant virtue: It works. It has attracted thousands of people to Jesus Christ and his church all across the country.

Spread three such calls on each prospect family by three different couples across a period of four to six weeks. Somewhere in this time span, stir in one call by the pastor. At the end of the sequence, add one decision call—ask them to transfer membership or make a primary decision for Christ. Keep making a high volume of these calls each week, especially on families who visit your worship service. Many of those on whom you call will soon become active members and leaders.

Making an Evangelistic Call

1. Get out of the car.

2. Go to the door (hardest part).

3. Knock or ring bell, whichever applies. If you cannot decide which, you are not competent enough to make evangelism calls. Get back in your car. Go home and go to bed. It is not safe for you to be on the streets. But if you are capable of making this basic decision, you can probably make a good evangelism call.

4. "Mrs. Jones?" You usually know the names of the people you are calling on. You may even have a card in the car which tells you a little about these folks.

5. Introduce yourself.

6. "We're calling for First Christian Church. We'd like to take a few minutes to get acquainted with you folks." Then shut up. They almost always let you in the house. What else can you do with someone from a church who says that on your front doorstep?

Many church members believe that people resent church callers. Wrong! Not unless the caller is obnoxious and rude. People appreciate courteous friendly calls. After all, it is solid evidence that someone cares about them. And who doesn't appreciate being cared about, especially in this impersonal, lonely society?

Statistics show that only one out of every four hundred calls will end up unpleasantly. And these few slammed doors *never* happen if people have already visited the church. The 1/400 ratio appears only in "cold turkey" calling, like going door-to-door in whole city blocks. Even then, the door slamming usually isn't from something offensive about the caller. It generally comes from some situation going on inside the house. Perhaps the marriage is coming apart. The couple has arrived at the zenith of a terrible quarrel. Just before you knock on the front door, she throws a toaster at him. He replies with an uncomplimentary remark. So he arrives at the front door in an angry mood. And now he has somebody to take it out on who can't fight back.

The middle-aged adolescent accounts for most other bad calls. As a child he had a poor relationship with his parents, especially his father. Often, he was forced to go to church every time the doors opened. So he said to himself during those years, "I'll show him. When I grow up, I'll never set foot inside a church again." So he spends the rest of his life venting his leftover anger on church callers. He isn't really mad at the caller; he's mad at his father.

7. What are your objectives once you are in the home? Most people don't know. That's why they feel so clumsy about making calls. And if they finally get up the courage to make a call, that's why they aren't sure whether they did it right. Nobody has ever told them exactly what they are there for.

a. To get acquainted. Personal relationships build the first bridge over which God's spirit begins to move into a person's life. God influences some people, like Moses, through a burning bush. Others find their life dramatically changed by the blinding light of some modern Damascus Road. A few may be converted by looking at a test tube or a sunset. But not many. Most Christians have never seen a burning bush in their backyard. Have you? But has God used some individual to influence your life? Think back to the time God first began to draw you to himself. Was that through an event? Or does the face of some individual spring from your memory banks? God begins that way for most people—through the personality of another person. Until that happens, nothing can happen. And we all know how to get acquainted with people. We do it all the time. Almost every day we meet somebody new. The evangelism call intends to accomplish much more than just getting acquainted. But if it doesn't accomplish that, it will accomplish little else.

b. To learn more about their religious interests. You don't sit there with a checklist asking questions and writing down the answers. You do it in the context of normal conversation. Is this a divided church home denominationally? What is their church background? Where did they live before they moved here? How long have they lived in town? Did they go to the Presbyterian Church when they lived in Louisiana? How old are their children?

c. To witness to your faith *in whatever way is natural for you.* In recent years the word "witness" has been mud splattered by various faulty definitions. Some think that a witness grabs people by the sleeve and says, "Are you saved?" He then delivers some kind of verbal karate chop and converts them on the spot. Occasionally, that may work. But most people do not respond to that approach, at least not positively. More often, they respond with nausea and retreat.

How do you witness to your faith? Even before you open your mouth, you have already used the strongest form of witness—your presence. You are there. Your physical presence in that home says, "We care about you. We care enough to send the very best, which is ourselves."

People witness verbally in various ways. Your personality, past religious experiences, and theological stance will determine what feels natural to you. Some people witness by bragging about their preacher. "We really do like our minister. His sermons have been very helpful to me." That is a powerful witness. Advertising experts say that nothing exerts a stronger influence than a satisfied customer.

Other people witness naturally by speaking about the warmth of their congregation. "We really have a good bunch of folks down there. I think you would enjoy them. We sure have a great time together." That kind of witness says in a powerful way, "Hey, this means something to me; it might mean something to you."

Other people witness by telling what God and their church experience means to them. They may have had an unusual spiritual pilgrimage, and they can speak about this in a moving way. If you can do that comfortably, great. But most people can't. They feel unnatural and egotistical with this kind of witnessing. Their spiritual experiences are too personal to talk about. Others have been taught in childhood that "Your spiritual life and your sex life are like your checking account; you don't discuss them with strangers." So don't feel that you have to witness in this way. If it feels natural, do it. If it doesn't, don't.

Other people witness naturally by describing the views of their congregation. One caller says, "I was a Baptist and my husband was a Methodist. We couldn't find a church home where we were both happy. Then we started attending First Christian. Their freedom of belief on doctrinal matters allows us to be satisfied with the same denomination." What a powerful witness, especially if the couple she is speaking with comes from two different backgrounds.

What is a witness anyway? Where do we get the word? From the New Testament. But they snatched it from the courtroom. What do court witnesses do? They make the case more believable. And very rarely does a single witness make the whole case. Several witnesses are usually brought in—perhaps a long list. A witness is never the judge and jury too. Nor does a witness need to know everything about the case. He knows what he knows, and that's all he has to tell. A Christian witness does the same. He makes the case for Jesus Christ more credible. He makes God's love more believable. So we don't need to know the whole Bible. We don't need to know *everything* about the church, theology, or our denominational beliefs. We just need to know what we know personally. And we already know that.

A lawyer in the Texas panhandle said, "I wish I could get my witnesses to understand that. I always tell them that before we go into court—you don't have to know everything, so don't try to know everything. That other lawyer will cross you all up in it and make you look like a fool. Just know what you know and nothing else when you get up on that stand."

Whatever way you choose to witness, try to avoid canned sermons and set spiels. These taste more like bologna than steak to most people. Respond to their interests and questions. Treat them personally, not programmatically. Nobody cares to be number 744 on a list of people to whom you have given your memorized witnessing speech.

d. Urge them to visit your church. Say this toward the end of the visit, perhaps as you are leaving. By doing it then, they won't misunderstand it as the prelude to a long sermon or a living room altar call. Some samples of how to say it:

"We sure would like to have you visit our church."
"Can we expect to see you in church this Sunday?"
"We appreciate you folks coming to church last week. We sure hope you will come back next Sunday."

Some callers erroneously think this invitation need not be put into words. "After all, they know why we came to see them." Wrong! The people being called upon could just as easily think, "They came to get acquainted, but they didn't invite us to church. Maybe they didn't like us."

Before leaving, give them a printed card describing the church. Keep it small, not more than 4" ×6", so it can fit into a pocket or purse. Otherwise, you go to the home looking like a Fuller Brush salesman. The card helps in many ways. It provides service times, street address, and a bit about the denominational viewpoint. But most important of all, it leaves a spot commercial in the home. Every house in America has a special purgatory for printed matter. Locations vary—the TV set, the dining room table, the kitchen cabinet, the refrigerator top, or the sink drawer. But someplace in the home lies a stack of undecidables—material too good to throw away and not good enough to keep. And every time family members sort through that pile, that card reminds them of your church. So don't spare the cost of printing. Make it look high quality. People don't quickly throw away an embossed card.

Most people make up their mind far more slowly than we expect. So a few weeks later when they finally decide to attend, they can't remember what time the service starts. "Didn't those callers leave a card with the times on it?" she asks. "Where did we put it?" So they hunt it up. Don't expect people to remember to look in the yellow pages. Many don't know that worship times are often printed there. Nor are they likely to call the church and ask.

Several Christian Churches (Disciples of Christ) throughout the United States and Canada have had good response from using a 4″ × 6″ card with the following information on it. Strangers to their congregation have been impressed by the positive way it introduces them to that denomination.

Example 1: Church Calling Card

Front

A picture or line drawing of the church building, the address, the name, and the times of services. The more simplicity and white space, the better. Don't crowd it with details; they get those if they start attending.

Back

Who Are We?

First Christian Church members are a cross-section of the community. Here people of every background and theology gather in a church whose basic belief is that every person must follow Christ as they personally see fit and personally understand the New Testament.

We are part of an American Christian movement which feels that denominational affiliation is not nearly as important as personal faith. We firmly believe that each individual's faith is so personal that we cannot rigidly demand that they affirm certain dogmatic ideas and deny others. Therefore, we readily welcome people from all denominations regardless of previous affiliation or present doctrinal convictions.

The basic thinking of our church might be summarized as follows:
1. Unity of all Christians through their common faith in Jesus Christ.
2. Freedom of thought on matters of doctrine.
3. Love and acceptance among all Christian people.
4. Cooperation among all denominations to achieve goals toward which all are working.

One of our early slogans was, "In essentials, unity; in non-essentials, freedom; in all things, love." This is still our basic plea today. We strive for the unity of Christian people in Jesus Christ as head of his body, the church, and for Christian love and cooperation between churches in spite of their differences of belief. We can tolerate a great divergence of theology within our congregation, since we do not consider the belief in certain doctrines or dogmas a necessity for salvation as do many other churches.

When calling on people who have never visited the church, always say as you hand them the card, "You do know where the church is located?"

(Unless they have already attended; if so, you can assume that they know how to get back.)

No matter how they answer this question, always describe the location. (Some nod yes, but give you a glassy-eyed look which betrays absent knowledge.) So always pinpoint the church visually in their head. If the street is a main thoroughfare, an address may be sufficient. In other cases, "just south of the courthouse" makes more sense. Callers from one congregation always say, "north of the Whataburger on 50th Street." Everybody in town instantly knows that location.

After leaving the home, make a notation on the *Prospect Record* of pertinent information. This will be invaluable to the pastor and future callers. Not in front of the house, of course, or on the front lawn. Pull down the street or around the block. Note your name, the date of the call, and how it went. Samples: "They are really interested in the church; They should be contacted by the young adult group; He might be interested in the men's softball team; They are interested in a strong youth group for their junior high daughter."

Every church needs some kind of printed record card. Types vary widely, but callers are much more likely to make notes on printed cards than on blank ones. The 4″ × 6″ form on the next two pages can be filed by last names in the upper left; or it can be used to sort cards geographically, using the street names in the upper right. The blanks on the back encourage each caller to make helpful comments.

If they turn out not to be prospects, indicate that on the card. But remember that they are prospects until proven otherwise. In early calls, it is often impossible to tell. So don't rule people out until they rule themselves out. People who aren't interested usually say so in definitive ways. "I think we'll probably go down to the Lutheran Church. We've always been Lutherans." That's a polite way of saying, "We're not interested." People are never harsh about this; but they are usually clear. So if they don't define themselves as uninterested, don't make judgments about their future behavior.

One pastor describes an experience which brought a turning point in his understanding of this principle. "I was calling one evening during a spring evangelism emphasis. One of our members had handed me a name obtained from a community telephone census. 'John, I really think you ought to go see her,' she said. 'This lady sounded upset on the phone. I somehow feel that they need a call from a minister.'

"It was a terrible night, thirty degrees with misting rain glazing everything a pale white. Already cold, I got out of my Volkswagen in front of the house. That machine was a torture chamber for winter calling in a city. It never got warm between houses. The strong wind whipped the elm trees and added sting to a few sleet crystals mixed with the mist. I knocked on the front door, which didn't have a stoop over it. A light glimmered faintly far back in the house. No answer. I knocked again. Waited a long time. Nobody came. Knocking again, my imagination began to smell the coffee waiting for me at the church. But as I turned to leave, the door

Example 2: Prospect Record

Front

MASTER PROSPECT RECORD

Family's Last Name _____ Address _____

Phone _____

First Name	Approx. Age	Occupation	Denominational Background
Miss			
Mr.			
Mrs.			

Children living at home   Hobbies or Interests:

1. _____   _____
2. _____   _____
3. _____   Other: _____
4. _____

Dates attended church: 1. _____ 2. _____ 3. _____

Directions for finding house: _____

Back

RECORD OF VISITATIONS

Called on by ——————————— date ———————————

Comments ————————————————————

Called on by ——————————— date ———————————

Comments ————————————————————

Called on by ——————————— date ———————————

Comments ————————————————————

Called on by ——————————— date ———————————

Comments ————————————————————

made squeaking sounds. A little gray-haired lady poked her head through a narrow opening. She made no motions to unlock the screen door that separated us. I engaged her in conversation, using my sparkling conversational manner. But she didn't let me in the house.

"Mrs. White was vocal and lengthy. If set in type, her animated conversation would have significantly increased the newsprint shortage. Meanwhile, I struggled to restrain my cold knees from knocking together. As more time passed, I began to feel angry. She stood there inside a cozy warm house. I was turning into an ice covered stalagmite. The next thing that happened was thirty more minutes of the same thing. During that time I learned that she was sixty-seven years old, having moved to our town when she was fourteen. She had been a member of our denomination in Kansas, apparently a bit slow in transferring her membership.

"Finally, the conversation over, I moved my frozen joints arthritically toward the car. Shaking the ice off my raincoat, I climbed into my deep-freeze Volkswagen. As I started down the street, I reached over and picked up Mrs. White's Prospect Record card. Crumpling it up angrily, I threw it into the trash container. About a block down the street I had a bad feeling. I think some churches call it 'being convicted of sin.' So I picked it out of the chewing gum wrappers and crumpled sales tickets and smoothed it out flat again. Another block down the street, I was once again overcome with anger. So I threw it away again. The next time I retrieved it, I lectured myself: 'You have to stick by your own rules. She didn't really say no. She sure didn't sound like a hot prospect, but she didn't rule us out.'

"A couple of weeks later we sent some lay people back to call. They got in the house. That made me more angry. But the next time I called, I got in the house. Within a few weeks, Mrs. White joined the church, wanting to be baptized. She became a regular attender and a tither. What a great experience for her and for me. Five years later, I officiated at her funeral service. Had I operated on my own feelings that night, both of us would have missed a great experience. So don't make judgments about the potential value of prospects. You can't always predict what they may do later. People don't change their minds very fast. Unless they say 'no' in clear terms, don't say 'no' for them or for God. You take care of your business—faithful calling. Let God take care of his. You cannot always tell by the outside package whether God is renovating people on the inside."

Never, never, never keep a Prospect Record overnight (unless you are using the Sunday morning Reach Out Team meeting described later in this chapter). Failure to return cards to the church after calling usually results in a malfunctioning record system and a nervous breakdown for leaders. Even if the people are home that evening and the first call gets made, record cards end up in the other purse (the one they didn't bring tonight), the other car (the one they didn't drive), the other suit (the one they didn't wear or the one at the cleaners), in the glove compartment, over the sun visor, under the seat, or "I can't remember where I put that."

Helpful Tips to Increase Caller Self-Confidence

1. Don't tell them where you got their name unless they ask. People who have already attended church never ask this question. And even on "cold turkey" calls, it only happens one out of seventy times. But if it does, don't say, "We got your name from a religious census." This makes the call seem cold and impersonal—the opposite of your intention. A better answer: "Our evangelism department works hard to get the names of people who might be interested in our church." Nobody ever probes that blanket reply with another question.

2. Don't talk theology. Few people bring up theology anyway. Why would they? That would let you find out how little theology they know, so they won't raise the subject.

One exception: That rare individual who has "The Religious Debating Syndrome." This person loves to *discuss* Christianity. He would rather argue religion than watch the Superbowl on TV. He doesn't mean anything bad by it—just loves to tangle people up in complicated theological arguments.

This type often begins by asking something like, "Now, what does your church really believe about baptism? Is that for the remission of sins?" Then come other questions. He meets each of your answers with a hairsplitting exception to your opinion. Hairsplitting leads to atom splitting. You finally leave at eleven o'clock feeling that little was accomplished.

How do you win with someone like that? By not playing the game. "I think I know the answer to that. But it might be better if you discussed it with our pastor. He could probably deal with it better than I can." You can thus dispatch something in one minute which could have wasted three hours.

This answer would not, of course, apply to simple inquiries like, "Do you baptize by immersion? What time is church? Do you have communion every Sunday?" You can field those. Use it for complex questions which scare the wits out of you—you think you ought to know, but you aren't sure that you do—or you aren't sure the asker is making an *honest* inquiry.

3. Don't get discouraged if several calls end up as nonprospects. In churches operating thorough calling programs, this happens frequently.

4. Don't stay long. One pastor in a rapidly growing church says, "Fifteen minutes is plenty. If you stay more than thirty minutes, you probably shouldn't have gone at all." Everyone has a vague mental plan for how they will spend their evening. During the day, she has been thinking, *I'm going to cut out that dress pattern for Susie tonight. This will be my last chance before the party on Friday.* He has been thinking, *I'm going to fix that darned lawn mower.* Or he may have been thinking, *I'm bushed. I'm going to relax tonight and watch TV.*

So you come calling that same evening. You have a great visit. You feel that they genuinely like you and enjoy the conversation. Time slides quickly by, and you leave at 9:00 P.M. after staying two hours. As the husband shuts the door behind you, he glances at the hall clock and realizes what time it is. Turning to his wife, he says with a sigh, "Well, that shoots the evening." Your fine call has impacted negatively because you committed grand larceny—you stole a whole evening.

Some church members use the same logic with calls that they use with their physician's prescriptions: "If one pill is good, five should really help." Others have a more subtle reason for staying too long. "What a good visit," they think. "If I stay a while longer, I won't have to make another call this evening. It'll be too late. I can just go on back to the church." This is the devil whispering in your ear. Don't listen.

5. *Don't try to visit if they have company.* When you see that they have guests, say, "We don't want to intrude on your evening. We'll call another time." If they insist that you come in anyway, insist that you will come another time. Make the mistake of going in, and you always encounter an unproductive relationship mix. You make the other guests feel awkward, and they make you feel awkward.

6. *Don't high pressure or mention joining the church.* Just urge them to attend. People rarely respond to pressure cooker tactics anyway. They respond to love and concern. Isn't that what you respond to?

This doesn't mean that you should *never* ask people to join the church. You should. Have three different couples make three different calls over a period of four to six weeks. During that time, the family will often start attending church (or continue to attend if they have already started). After that, someone should visit to ask them for a decision. With a few individuals, special reasons demand that you wait several months before a decision call. But such exceptions are about as rare as ostrich eggs in Nebraska. If you don't ask them to join, most people will move like a ship toward the harbor, then past it. You have turned their mind's attention toward Christ; then lost it by not giving them the opportunity to make a permanent decision.

Presence, proclamation, and persuasion—these three keys influence people toward Christ. The type of calling discussed in this chapter accomplishes the first two. But without the third key, all other effort withers to uselessness. Some people, of course, take the initiative themselves. They join without being asked. But most don't.

What keeps people from making a final decision? In order of importance, the following factors:

   a. Nobody asked them
   b. Procrastination
   c. Crowd fear
   d. Fear of baptism procedures
   e. Misunderstanding about baptism requirements of your denomination
   f. Misunderstanding about membership transfer process

A few churches make the opposite mistake. They rush in to *persuade* before presence and proclamation have accomplished their work. Such timing is like icing a cake before you bake it. But most church leaders neglect the decision call completely, so the cake is never completed.

Who should make the decision call? The pastor or someone knowledge-able in that kind of calling. Probably not more than 1 percent of church members feel comfortable in this type of call. But that's fine. Ninety-nine percent of all evangelism calling doesn't include asking for a decision anyway.

7. Learn more about their religious interests sometime during the conversation. Don't get totally sidetracked by the snowstorm, the rainstorm, the Dallas Cowboys, or the price of groceries. Such topics rarely monopolize the entire conversation anyway, so this is seldom a problem. From courtesy or curiosity, people usually change the subject to religion. So you won't need a memorized formula for getting into it.

8. Do not preach. Most churches pay someone to do this for twenty minutes every Sunday morning. People expect sermons to occur there, not in their living room.

9. Do not try to outtalk the TV. Some nights you just can't win. Monday, for example, football night. So don't set Monday as a regular calling night. No church visitor can compete with that attention getter.

Talking low sometimes helps. They keep having to ask you to repeat what you just said. Finally, they turn it down or off. In some instances the caller may say, "I'll bet I'm interrupting one of your favorite programs." This gentle statement usually pulls them back to the real world.

10. Treat evangelism prospects like anyone else you meet for the first time. We all know how to meet people. We do it every day. You probably met a new person this past week. Did your anxiety level increase a bit? Yes, you fumbled for some words. But you lived through it, didn't you? Evangelism calling requires exactly the same skills you used then.

11. Relax and be yourself. If you can relax, they can too. Some people on whom you call have previously been victims of a very different type call. So they are waiting for you to sprinkle sawdust on their carpet and make your altar call. When that doesn't happen, they drop their defensive stance and appreciate your presence.

12. If someone resists your call, back off. Christ stands at the door and knocks; he doesn't hit it with a battering ram. Unless they are mentally willing to relate, you won't get anywhere anyway.

13. What time of day should you call? Mostly in the evening, when both husband and wife are home. Single persons furnish obvious exceptions to this rule.

14. Should you telephone in advance? Generally, no. Two hour visits without prior notice break all social codes. But fifteen minutes doesn't destroy an evening. Then too, some people will put you off over the phone by saying, "Maybe it would be better if you come by some other time." If they say the same thing next week, you will begin feeling awkward about making the call. You even begin to feel awkward about *telephoning* again. But had you gone directly to their front door, a good relationship might have developed. Their fear of religious fanatics would have dissolved immediately.

In a few communities you must phone ahead because people fear for their personal safety. But most calls, especially first-time contacts, work better without advance arrangements. If you don't believe this, try five calls this way and five calls your way. That tells you what works best in your town.

15. Negative people get negative results. Someone asked, "Is there any kind of person who should not make evangelism calls?"

Answer: "Yes, the type of church member who was baptized in dill pickle juice." Some Christians compulsively tell everyone how bad things are at the church. Put them to work at record keeping or coffee preparation. Anything to keep them out of the calling cadre.

The hostess in a motel dining room greeted a young couple. "Would you like to go through our buffet?" she asked.

"Is it good?" the young man replied.

"I don't know," the hostess said.

After a brief conversation, the couple decided against the buffet. Similarly, church salesmen who infer only bad news about their wares attract few customers.

16. Enthusiasm generates interest. A minister sat by a pretty blond girl on a flight to Dallas. They didn't talk, but he couldn't help noting her engagement ring—she kept twisting it back and forth to catch the sparkle of the evening sun pouring through the window. As the plane landed, she looked out beyond the wing tip with anticipation.

"Does your fiancé live in Dallas?" the minister asked her, breaking a fifty-minute silence.

"How did you know that?" she said with a startled grin.

"Just guessing," he replied.

What kind of attitude do *you* take along on an evangelism call? You probably won't reach that girl's excitement pitch, but most of us could stand to adjust our enthusiasm level upward at least two notches. How can anyone become enthusiastic about our church if we aren't?

17. Calling equals caring. Evangelism calling begins with *caring about Jesus Christ*. If we don't find Christ helpful in our own life, we won't care about evangelism.

Secondly, evangelism calling means we *care enough about people* to want them to find Christ. Just caring about people doesn't necessarily motivate us to do evangelism. The medical profession contains plenty of personnel who genuinely care about people. Counselors care about people. But Philip and Paul cared about people enough to help them encounter Jesus Christ. A retired minister described a sermon title he saw on a church bulletin years ago: "If in the Twentieth Century a Man Dies and Goes to Hell, Whose Business Is It and Who Cares?" Few would phrase our motivation for evangelism that way today. But caring whether people find the Christ experience is still the church's basic business. People need God in their life more than they need most other things. Jesus was right when he said that life does not consist of bread alone (Matthew 4:4). But some of us who grew up in the church have never tried to live on just bread alone. So we don't fully understand the hunger people have for "something more." And that keeps us from reaching out to them with the bread of life—Jesus Christ.

Thirdly, evangelism calling means we care enough about people to *make personal contact with them.* Some fear that our evangelism will appear either foolish or offensive (as to the Greeks and Jews in 1 Corinthians 1:23). More often, it does neither—it doesn't even get their attention. "Nor do men light a lamp and put it under a bushel. . ." Jesus said (Matthew 5:15). But church people do that all the time. We hide our light—Christ—under the church organization. Evangelist calling programs seek to reverse that selfishness. They thrust the light toward the dark corners of people's lives.

In the movie *Oh God,* John Denver plays a grocery store manager to whom God appears. The first time this happens, Denver is taking a shower. In the animated conversation which follows, Denver asked George Burns (who plays God), "Do you really expect people to believe that you exist?"

George Burns replies for God, "That's your job. Get the word out."

Newcomer Calling

This procedure varies considerably from the type of call mentioned above. If possible, avoid going into the house. You consume too much time with too few results. With a bit of experience you can make eight newcomer calls per hour. But go into the house each time and that figure reduces to one or two per hour. When people urge you to come in, say, "I know you are busy and I don't want to take up too much of your time." (Avoid saying that you have several more calls to make. This makes the visit seem cold and impersonal. It also implies that other people are more important than they are.)

Begin by introducing yourself and asking, "Are you folks getting settled?" This usually brings a lengthy response of some kind. How bad it was to move—how many things the movers broke! Any caller can sympathize with this. He knows what it's like to move, and this ice-breaker helps the conversation start flowing.

After these initial pleasantries run down, ask, "Have you folks found a church home here in Bartonsville yet?" This question produces a sometimes brief, sometimes lengthy, response. But it always tells you many things about their religious background and feelings. It usually brings natural opportunities for additional questions and further information interchange.

If they have already settled on a church, say, "We don't want to take anyone away from a church of their choice. We're glad to have you in the community. If we can ever be of any help to you, let us know." Then exit.

If they have not yet affiliated with a church, say, "We sure would like to have you visit our church." Then tell them a little about it, and perhaps a bit about yourself. You would particularly emphasize the programs in which you think they might have interest.

In either case, always leave them a card describing the church location and service times. You can never tell which people may change their minds later. After all calls, note pertinent information on the Prospect Record card: The date, your initials, opinions about whether they are prospects, and other important family facts.

But what if they aren't newcomers to town? Perhaps you have insufficient information to know whether they are really prospects. Or what if you are calling house to house in whole city blocks? Begin as above by introducing yourself. Then move directly to the question, "Do you folks have a church home here in town?" Then respond to their answer in the same manner described above for newcomers.

Exception: The infrequently encountered "yes-no" syndrome person. This individual always answers questions with a yes or no rather than engaging in conversation. So even at the close of the call, you still can't be sure about them. Try asking casually, "Have you folks been acquainted with the Christian Church (substitute the name of your denomination) in the past?"

This question nearly always brings a flood of information about their religious background. Some may say, "Yes, my uncle is a Christian Church preacher in Indiana." Others will tell you that they attended your denomination when they lived in California. Still others will say, "No, we are Mormons!" However they respond, the answer usually always defines their prospect status and provides good information.

If newcomers talk like they are interested prospects, but don't respond by attending, keep the Prospect Record. File it in a separate file. Check back again a year later. They may respond at that time. Seven preachers may visit during the family's first two weeks in town. But after that, most churches drop them and never call again. This procedure overlooks the fact that many people make church selections slowly. They do everything else first—electricity, gas, dentist. Then they get around to serious thinking about a church. By that time, most churches have given up on them.

Calling in the Small Church

Several smaller congregations have had good success by using the following system to call on everyone who visits their worship services. It gets the job done effectively with almost no organizational red tape. Gather your calling couples together at a meeting and read them the following plan.

1. Philosophy of Reach-Out Calling: "Go therefore and make disciples of all nations. . ." Jesus tells us (Matthew 28:19). "So we are ambassadors for Christ, God making his appeal through us," Paul says (2 Corinthians 5:20). "But you shall receive power when the Holy Spirit has come upon you; and you shall be my witnesses in Jerusalem and in Judea and Samaria and to the end of the earth," Jesus says (Acts 1:8). Our community is part of the world which God so loved. The people who live here have deep needs which can only be met by Jesus Christ. God will empower us with his Spirit when we try to be his ambassadors in making new disciples.

2. The Goals of Reach-Out Calling: Our goal is not just to add new members to the church, though that will certainly happen as a secondary result. Our first goal is to respond to all worship service visitors with the kind of warmth and friendliness which will encourage them to make a positive decision for Jesus Christ. A second goal is the renewal of spiritual enthusiasm and commitment to the task of evangelism among members of the congregation. A third goal is the general education of church leaders regarding successful methods for winning people to Jesus Christ.

3. The Plan for Reach-Out Calling: Studies continue to show that repetitive personal contact between nonmembers and members is the most important single factor in church growth. All growing congregations have some simple system for reaching out to nonmembers with friendly interest. The Reach-Out Calling Team is a simple way to implement this necessity.
FIRST WEEK, select and recruit couples who will make up the Reach-Out Calling Team (don't ask for volunteers—select people).
SECOND WEEK, train the couples (study this chapter together, or read pertinent parts of this chapter onto a cassette tape and play it for the group as a basis for a training discussion).
THIRD WEEK, recognize and dedicate the team couples in the morning worship service.
FOURTH WEEK, begin a five to ten minute meeting of all calling team couples between Sunday school and morning worship service. The group will continue meeting *every* Sunday for the entire year. At these meetings they will report to each other on calls made during the past week and receive new assignment cards for calls to be made during the coming week. A total of four calls during four consecutive weeks will be made on every person who visits the worship services (or becomes a prospect through other sources). The pastor makes the first call during the first week after they visit for the first time. Then three different calls will be made by three different calling team couples during the next three consecutive weeks. This consecutive calling rotation should continue with each prospect until all three calls have been made, or until they have joined the church, or until they have indicated that they are not interested in the church, whichever comes first. The three consecutive calls should be made even if the prospects don't attend church the second and third Sundays after they visit the first time.
EIGHTH WEEK, etc., the pastor makes a decision call sometime after the first four basic calls have been completed, using his own judgment about whether they are ready for such a call. The pastor would not ordinarily ask

people for a decision unless they have started attending church services. NINTH WEEK, etc., the Team Chairperson arranges for each family who has joined the church to be called on by three different couples from an adult Sunday school class (and/or the teacher of an appropriate children's class) during three consecutive weeks, with the objective of getting them acquainted with more people and getting them involved in the Sunday school program.

4. The Organization for Reach-Out Calling: Couples who make up the team will work under the leadership of a chairperson who will meet with the team each week between Sunday school and morning worship, receive their reports of calls made, and assign appropriate calls for the following week. Each couple ordinarily makes only one call per week, but may be asked to make more than one if the need arises.

5. The Key to Success: Personal responsibility and attention to details are the keys to success at all phases. The team *must* meet every week. The pastor *must* make the call the first week after people visit the first time. The team members *must* make their assigned calls each week, otherwise the system breaks down into uselessness. Couples who cannot attend a Sunday meeting *must* telephone the chairperson *prior* to Sunday and report on their call so that he can make out a duplicate card to be assigned to another couple at the Sunday team meeting. If a team couple does not show up for the Sunday meeting, but fails to telephone him in advance to report their call and indicate that they will be absent, he *must* call them on Sunday evening and obtain the information he needs in order to make that particular call himself *that week* so that the rotation will not be lost. This approach to evangelism is not easy; it is demanding and challenging. But if the program is followed in meticulous detail, the rate of those joining the church will increase radically over last year's totals.

Whatever methods are used, nothing compensates for a high volume of repetitive personal contacts. An insurance salesman earned one of his company's annual sales awards. He had sold more life insurance than any other agent in the state. The company president traditionally presented this award at the annual state convention. At that time, the winner always made a brief speech, telling his success secrets. Unfamiliar with public speaking, the salesman worked long and hard on his acceptance speech. Writing it out line by line, he memorized it each morning while shaving. After two weeks, he had it grooved into his brain like a record.

The night of the big convention arrived. The time came for the top sales awards. The president made a great introduction, honoring his achievement and concluding by calling him forward. After shaking hands for the camera and giving him a gold plaque, the company chief handed him the microphone. The nervous salesman turned to face that great sea of eyes, all waiting expectantly for his advice. His computer blanked. He couldn't think of word one; he couldn't even think of word two. "Uh. . .uh. . .uh . . ." he said, trying to find the beginning. Finally he remembered something from down in the middle. Anywhere, he thought. Start anywhere. "See the people," he said with relieved enthusiasm. But he couldn't remember what came next. "Uh. . .uh. . .uh. . ." he continued. "See the people. . .," he said again. Failing once more at finding the starting line, he repeated it again: "Uh. . .uh. . .uh. . .see the people!" Totally embarrassed, he sat down.

But some thought it was a perfect speech. He said it all.

We can't compare influencing people toward Christ with selling insurance. Evangelism efforts challenge people to make a decision about who will be Lord of their life. That choice has far broader implications than buying life insurance. But one factor correlates identically. If you want your church to grow, you'll have to do that too—see the people.

An old story tells of Jesus arriving in heaven after his resurrection. Gabriel meets him at the gate and asks, "Who will carry on your work now that you are gone from the earth?"

Jesus replies, "I have called Peter and John. They will carry out my work and tell others of me."

"But what if Peter and John don't tell anyone," Gabriel replies. "What is your plan then?"

"I have no other plan," Jesus says.

"Our people feel we can have a good church without good youth work, but not a great church."

7 Those Kids Would Drive Me Crazy

How to Maintain a Strong Youth Program

Two hundred forty-eight board members from thirty-eight local congregations of the Christian Church (Disciples of Christ) were asked to rank their top five priorities for the next five years. When all the scores were combined, "New Models for Meeting Youth Needs" came in second out of forty-two choices on the list. When asked to name the strongest churches in their local community, many laymen added, "I understand they really have a going organization over there. They sure have a lot of stuff happening for young people."

One man explained this high interest in youth programming like this: "Sunday school attendance in most churches has significantly declined since about 1955. So the 'going youth group' has now replaced the 'going Sunday school' as a symbol of success in many of our churches."

Another person said, "Our people feel that we can have a *good* church without good youth work, but not a *great* church."

But what a dilemma this creates for leaders. They *want* good youth groups, but are seldom able to make them a reality. Knowledgeable sponsors seem impossible to locate. Parents and church fathers often disagree on what activities the youth should engage in. Many groups launch with a high flame of enthusiasm in September, but die down to low attendance and extinction by Halloween.

Why all this confusion? Sunday school programs seem to run themselves. Why can't youth work? Mostly because church leaders don't grasp the underlying principles of success in this task. Those desiring to play tennis must master some basic principles if they intend to win any games. So it is with youth work.

The following list provides this information. Regardless of time, place, size of group, or denomination, these fundamentals produce healthy youth groups. Many key church leaders will never serve as youth sponsors; but they must understand the principles. Otherwise, how can they set appropriate policies to undergird the programs?

1. Use the right combination of sponsors. Two couples working together make the best possible combination. Other alternatives include a couple and a single adult, or two singles. This two family unit arrangement automatically eliminates a major youth work problem—loneliness. Picture yourself and your spouse all alone at the church every Sunday evening—no other adults around. You soon begin to feel, "We are down here taking care of everyone else's kids while they are out for a drive, playing golf, or watching Sunday afternoon football. This isn't fair." Your loneliness leads to self-pity. The self-pity leads to low enthusiasm. The low enthusiasm turns to apathy. Next you find excuses for canceling meetings or failing to show up. This leads to feeling guilty and a middle of the year resignation.

But two couples working together make four adults. Junior and senior high groups meeting at the same time (in different parts of the building, of course) add up to at least eight adults. This combats empty church building blues. They feel like a team. They can talk with each other. They have fun together. So when you recruit sponsors, think of couples who appear compatible. Then you can say, "We are asking the Smiths to work with you. We think you would make a good team." Many more people will say "yes" to that approach than to a solitary confinement request.

An amateur golfer challenged his club pro to a match. "But," said the amateur, "you've got to give me a handicap of two got'chas."

The pro had no idea what a "got'cha" was, but he was confident and agreed to the terms. As they began to tee off, the pro prepared to swing. At that moment the amateur crept up from behind, grabbed him around the waist, and shouted, "Got'cha."

They finished the game without further incident, but the pro played terribly and was beaten. When someone asked why he had lost to a lesser player, he mumbled, "Have you ever played eighteen holes of golf waiting for a second got'cha?"

Sponsoring an evening youth group brings a similar challenge. Even experienced sponsors expect a few got'chas along the way. They wonder whether they can handle these adequately; they need someone to talk with, to think through problems with, and give them confidence. The two couple team creates this automatic emotional support system. Also, two different family units provide two different personality types. That gives two different perspectives on problems and adds balance to program planning.

This couple "buddy system" also minimizes detail work by the minister. Two couples working together tend to resolve most things between themselves. Instead of knocking on the pastor's door with every tiny problem, they work things out. That doesn't mean that the minister should not concern himself with youth work. In extremely small churches, he may even serve as a sponsor. He will carry active concern for youth in churches of every size. But increasing the self-reliance of lay leaders always beats clergy dependency. No pastor stays at a church forever. What happens to the clergy dominated youth program when he moves? Sometimes it dies from lack of trained sponsors.

The two-couple team also protects leaders from the Sunday evening time cage. Many potential sponsors say "no" in order to avoid getting tied up for every Sunday evening all year. But if two couples work together, they think, "If I have to go out of town, the other couple could meet with the group. That wouldn't be so bad. We might be able to handle that." Don't let the couples trade off each month. That destroys the program (for reasons to be discussed later). But an occasional absence of one couple creates no problem. And how differently that freedom makes sponsors feel. Put a parakeet in a cage with the door standing open all the time. Put another bird into a cage with the door locked. Which do you suppose feels the most comfortable about his confinement?

2. Pick sponsors who can communicate with youth. Teenagers often develop communication problems at home and these difficulties don't all originate with poor parenting; some come from a normal clash of generations and viewpoints. Young people must struggle through the self-limiting psychosis of adolescence; their parents hope to avoid the embarrassment of rearing children destined for the state penitentiary. Youth need and desire more freedom; parents feel highly responsible and have a hard time letting go. Conflict naturally results.

Capable youth sponsors can help ease this tension. Youth will often talk with them about personal problems and values. Unfortunately, few adults possess natural talents for communicating with teenagers. They lack openness and nonjudgmental attitudes. They hear only the superficial teenage conversational patter; they miss the hopes, dreams, and fears just below the surface. So pick sponsors with an eye for personal relationship skills, not biblical scholarship interests alone. At this age, adult role models often exert far more influence than the right Bible verse.

3. Select sponsors; don't ask for volunteers. Never advertise in the newsletter, "We desperately need sponsors and can't get anybody to do it." That is approximately like saying, "The only qualification you need is the willingness to volunteer. Any dummy can do this job. If you are any dummy, please volunteer." How would you feel about a job for which you were recruited in that way?

Out of any one hundred lay persons, less than five possess both the willingness and giftedness to work with youth. That makes the target group from which you can get sponsors very small. So start your process with that in mind. The question is never, "Who will do it?" The critical issue is, "How can we find those few persons who have the needed skills?"

Begin by meeting with the Christian education committee. Brainstorming together, decide on the qualities you think a youth sponsor needs. How can you decide who you want until you decide what kind of person they should be? One committee developed the following set of attributes they would like to see in a sponsor:

a. A responsible adult between the ages of twenty and retirement
b. Commitment to Jesus Christ as Lord and Savior
c. Emotionally stable
d. Able to relate well to youth
e. Able to relate in a positive way to other adults
f. Able to work as a team member with other adult leaders without trying to dominate
g. Able to deal with conflict and tensions in a positive way
h. A person who expresses the Christian faith in daily life

Next, review the church membership list, looking for persons who seem to fit these qualifications. And don't overlook people just because they exceed age thirty. Emotionally mature adults age forty to fifty sometimes make fine sponsors. They recognize all the silly stages that kids go through as just that—stages. This makes them much more relaxed around youth. They don't feel impelled to reform everybody. They accurately assess many teenage traits as potholes on the road to growing up.

Youth don't automatically respect sponsors close to their own age. They *do* respect sponsors who can relax around them, relate to them without being uptight, be kind but firm about keeping the group on the track, keep order most of the time, and promote a sense of fairness in all activities and relationships. Does the adult seem to have a gift for working with youth? Sign them up. Don't fuss about them being over thirty, or even forty. Attitude and skill count more than birth dates.

After developing a set of sponsor qualifications, mimeograph them on cards. Make an appointment to see the potential youth workers in person. Never recruit them over the phone. That signals them that you don't take this job very seriously. So they won't either. When you make the visit to their home, say something like this: "Our education committee is working on the selection of junior high sponsors for the new year. We feel that these are the qualities we would like the adults who work with our youth to have." Show them the card and read the points aloud with them. "The Christian Education committee feels that you are the kind of person who measures up to these standards."

Doesn't that have more impact than a casual want ad in a mimeographed newsletter? Realizing that they were selected by a committee adds real punch. They can't reject that request without considerable thought. Everyone finds it much harder to say no to a group than to one person.

Then tell them, "We know that you may feel that you don't know much about the youth program. But we want to assure you that you will be trained. We are holding a training session the evening of August _____ to make plans for the new year. You will receive materials at that time which will help you get started off in a good way. And you will not be alone in the job. We are asking two couples to work with each youth group this year. We don't mean that we want you to trade off for different weeks or months. That doesn't work well. But we do want you to know that in case you have to be out of town some weekend, you won't have the difficulty of finding a substitute that some sponsors have had in the past.''

Always tell them their exact responsibilities, such as meeting times and length of service expected—never more than one year. Then don't fail to deliver on your promise about the one year term. When you recruit for next year, give those who performed well an opportunity to work again. But don't take them for granted year after year until they scream, ''We want out!'' If sponsors must complain to you in order to get loose, they have probably already complained to several other church members. By now the whole church knows how hard the work is and how unending the tenure. Your lack of concern for sponsors thus sows negative seed throughout the congregation—especially in the age group from which you will need to recruit *new* sponsors. And those weed seeds will keep coming up for years afterward, making it increasingly difficult to find good adult leaders.

Asking sponsors each year whether they wish to sign up for another year helps in five ways: 1) It puts them in control of the decision; 2) They can withdraw in a graceful way at the time when they feel like it; 3) You can diplomatically ease them out of the program if they don't perform well the first year; 4) They tend to keep a more creative edge during the time of their service; and 5) Sponsor complaints don't poison the springs from which you must draw more sponsors.

How long should a sponsor serve? A few rare individuals can sustain keen ability with youth over a period of many years. But the productive life span of most good sponsors runs from three to five years. By this time they grow weary in their work. The razor edge of excitement about the new year has dulled to the sharpness of a rubber ball. Creativity wanes, enthusiasm declines; tiredness sets in like an all day rain. The youth, accurately sensing the sponsor's attitude, begin to feel the same way. Ideally, use two couples for each group—one experienced and one new couple—thus providing an automatic on-the-job training program. At the end of each year, evaluate which couples you should ask to serve again.

4. Use the same sponsors all year. One well-meaning pastor said, ''Let's use a different couple each month. With a rotation system, nobody will have to work very hard.'' The group fell apart in two months. Why? Kids don't relate to adults quickly. Not until they spend four to six hours together can they begin to feel at ease. That takes four to six weeks of youth meetings. At this point, kids differ little from adult groups. Their members seldom become comfortable with each other prior to six hours of dialogue. Only then can enough trust develop to produce honest and open discussions. So any group which changes leaders each month has planned its own funeral. Trust and communication simply don't develop in that climate. The group relationships blossom, but always die from frostbite before the fruit sets on.

5. Understand the purpose of evening youth groups. Sunday school and evening youth groups aim at identical targets—instilling and maturing faith in Jesus Christ. But the method for accomplishing this differs radically between the two. Sunday school relies largely on content-centered learning. Sunday evening programs use mostly experience-centered learning. What's the difference? Memorizing the multiplication tables in the fourth grade is content-centered learning. You learn by thinking about concepts. But learning to ride a bicycle in the fourth grade is experience-centered learning. You learn by doing.

Sunday school and youth groups compare similarly. Sunday evening can't substitute for Sunday morning, anymore than doing multiplication problems can replace memorizing the tables. But Sunday morning can't replace Sunday evening either. In youth groups, young people learn what it means to be the church by being the church. They learn skills which prepare them to serve on church boards as adults. They develop organizational and leadership talents which help them in all of life's group situations. And is not life mostly group activity? The John Wayne frontier days of rugged individualism died in the 1880s. So youth unprepared to work with other people in groups aren't prepared for life itself.

Youth work's most powerful influence probably lies in positive peer relationship development. After hearing a member criticize the frivolity of youth activities, a minister wrote the following article in his church paper:

Sunday a week ago, I spent the evening with our youth. Peggy is doing a fine job giving them the Christian leadership that is so important at this time in their lives. Coupled with this experience was a TV program called 'Who Killed Richie?' It is the true story of a promising young boy who was caught up in drugs and finally killed by his father, who was facing a possible attack by Richie with a knife. The program continued to raise the question of 'Who Killed Richie?' The peers and friends he chose, the activities he sought, the contacts he made, were all indicative of a definite direction. They became the seeds of a final scene that was destructive unto death.

I say all of this to give you a definite reason why our church invests so much in our youth. *Positive peer group activities do develop and influence the later directions of persons.* Last weekend our junior highs went on a trip to Ruidoso; and the high school youth had a garage sale. Our youth have opportunities to be in a handbell choir, a youth choir, or create a puppet ministry, all just for starters. Now some would raise the question of whether these are serious enough activities for our kids at church. But being a part of a positive fun youth activity is valuable for these formative years."[1]

Church members often berate the poor study material available from denominational presses. Sometimes they should. But peer group activities probably influence the young person's life far more than curriculum content. Not that study isn't important; it is. But the education received from print on paper shapes fewer lifetime goals than flesh and blood relationships. No study book molds life like working with Christian adults and youth, playing together, and being the church together.

6. Understand the value of out-of-town trips. "What do trips accomplish?" most church members ask. "Aren't they unnecessary?" But trips play irreplaceable roles in the total program. For one thing, they provide a shared experience which helps make the group a group. Whether you visit a denominational children's home or take a ski trip, the individuals return as a group. They have shared experiences which make their identity unique among other church groups.

Secondly, a trip forces members to relate to each other in new ways. Trapped together for a weekend, they get acquainted on deeper levels. Jim disliked Ken. They got into a fuss before, during, or after every meeting. But on the trip they had to ride in the same car, share a bathroom, and bunk together. Rubbing elbows and luggage struck sparks at first. But Jim also discovered that Ken had a few good qualities. They didn't return home bosom pals, but they can at least tolerate each other now. Attending meetings on Sunday evenings would never have produced that kind of experience.

Thirdly, trips create common goals for the group members. A trip is one of the most exciting things a kid can think about doing. So planning a weekend adventure in the fall instantly unifies the group. (Adults meet this need for a common goal by building buildings and conducting various kinds of campaigns.)

Fourthly, trips provide practice in decision making. No number of study programs on "sharing" or "cooperation" can substitute for a "live" experience on this subject. Will we go to the beach or the mountains? How will we spend our money when we get there? Hammering out these questions helps reconstruct give and take personalities out of take and take inclinations.

"Are kids who haven't attended meetings eligible to go on trips?" That question always comes up. "Can we bring a guest?" is another frequent inquiry. Settle it early in the fall, not during the heat of circumstances and personalities. Trip guests reduce the possibility of achieving a major goal of all trips—development of a strong group spirit. If several go who never attended Sunday meetings, the event accomplishes nothing except entertainment. Not only that, youth possess a strong sense of fairness. They don't appreciate people who skip the work and only show up for the fun. The youth can easily return more divided instead of more unified. At the beginning of the year, establish a rule. How many meetings must the kids attend in order to qualify for trips? "But can Betty go if she pays her own way?" someone will always ask. This sounds reasonable, but isn't. It fractures the "group building" process which trips try to accomplish.

At least a week prior to the trip, communicate with the parents *in writing*. Tell them the trip plans, leaving time, returning time, and what personal items youth should bring. Give the names of adult chaperons and a telephone number where the youth can be reached in emergencies. Parents usually get inaccurate and incomplete word-of-mouth communication from their children. So the thoughtfulness of a paper communiqué greatly increases parental cooperation and support.

7. *Make a strong beginning in the fall.* How your group takes off will determine how it flies all year. Get set to go full blast the first weekend after Labor Day. Don't start before that. The holiday weekend with its family trips and goof-off atmosphere will collapse your momentum. At that first meeting, start planning a trip for no later than November 1. This pulls the group together around an exciting common goal (especially helpful for those who come for the first time, and aren't sure whether they will return).

At the first meeting after returning from the fall trip, begin making plans for a spring trip. This counteracts the letdown feeling that comes to any group which has just completed a big goal. Keep calendaring things to which group members can look forward. Youth, like adults, run better on anticipation than on memories.

8. *Develop effective financing for youth work.* Church budgets usually support Sunday school programs. Class members don't raise money for curriculum with car washes and bake sales. But for Sunday evening Christian education, many church boards expect the groups to support themselves. Some congregations deal with this inequity by budgeting five hundred dollars per year for each group. This allows sponsors to make a stronger beginning in the fall. Without some arrangement of this sort, being broke strangles the immediate planning of trips and functions.

Groups should augment budget support with carefully selected money raising projects. These efforts produce common goals and improve group relationships by forcing people to work together. Generally speaking, one big project beats several smaller ones. One high school group does only one fund-raising project each year—a dinner theater in February. Rehearsal for this drama/eating production begins in early fall. More than one hundred youth get involved in some way: acting, props, meal preparation, serving tables. Everyone who attends buys a rather expensive ticket, even the youth themselves. But parents and other adults find the event worthwhile. They like it much better than six bake sales, three car washes, and umpteen garage sales. And it nets the group more than $2,000 annually.

9. *Understand that discipline problems are always a part of youth work.* During a simpler era, one denomination sought five qualities in the persons they selected for the foreign mission field. The candidate had to be: 1) physically strong; 2) emotionally stable; 3) mentally literate; 4) socially sensitive; and 5) spiritually compelled. Youth sponsors need approximately the same qualifications. They should have: the tireless energy of a bill

collector; the curiosity of a cat; the tenacity of a Boston bulldog; the self-assurance of a college sophomore; the determination of a New York taxi driver; the patience of a self-sacrificing wife on a too short budget; the enthusiasm of a rock music fan; the good humor of a Johnny Carson; and the diplomacy of someone who intends to referee a soccer game between the Jews and the Arabs. More than anything else, the sponsor understands that death, taxes, and discipline problems are always with him. Becoming a great youth sponsor doesn't mean that you eliminate all discipline problems; it means you learn to accept them as a normal part of life.

Every out-of-town trip produces at least one major discipline problem. Sponsors can never anticipate these; they always involve some totally crazy unexpected happening. Example: Eighteen junior highs go to the mountains for a weekend of playing in the snow. The event goes well. After lunch on Sunday, it's time to return home. Before they left on Friday, one boy's mother picked him up at school. Stopping by a shoe store, she bought him a new pair of $27.95 Red Wing boots to wear to the mountains. But at packing up time on Sunday afternoon, he can't find his boots.

What to do? Sponsors caucus. Obvious conclusions: "We cannot take Johnny home minus his $27.95 Red Wing boots. What would we say to his mother? We lost them in the snow?" Fortunately, one of the sponsors has some inside information. He knows that one of the kids has recently been in trouble for petty theft. Part of the sponsors organize an impromptu hiking experience. The other two sponsors search the luggage. Sure enough, they find the boots in the first suitcase they open.

Whenever a big problem like this arises on a trip, sponsors should talk with the parents immediately upon arriving home. Say something like, "We had a problem on the trip that I wanted to make you aware of. I think we have taken care of it. I don't think you need to take any further disciplinary action. But I felt that you would want us to let you know about it."

Always hold this conference with the parents *immediately* after returning to town. Do not wait until next week, or next month, or when you have more time. Before the sun sets that day, talk with those parents. Why? When the youth talks to them, he may distort the matter beyond all recognition. And he may paint you as the bad guy in the black hat instead of the good sponsor doing his best. After that, some parents remain forever blind to the truth in spite of all facts to the contrary. The danger compounds when the parents pass their distorted information along to other parents. After this happens, clearing the matter up is like trying to gather up a sack of feathers spread across a windy west Texas cotton field.

Most discipline problems at evening meetings relate to particular problem individuals. First, try all the standard techniques well known to public school teachers. Try giving him more attention. Appeal to his sense of fair play. Give him a leadership role. Make him captain of the debate or foozeball team. Sometimes the biggest problem causers make the best group leaders.

95

But after exhausting all these methods, some problems will remain. As with many adults, some youth get a larger emotional charge from creating trouble than from acting positive. These individuals must eventually be dealt with privately. At some opportune time, sit down with them alone and say something like this: "I'm concerned about your attitude. I feel like you are not happy in the group. You have continued to create various kinds of problems, and I'm really concerned about you. I just wanted to hear your side of it." Then shut up and listen. Sometimes they won't say much. Sometimes they say a lot. They get something off their chest, and you get to the root of the matter (which may be somewhere other than you expected). Either way, the opportunity to talk and your willingness to listen often improves their behavior.

But what if none of these routines work and the youth becomes intractably belligerent? One sponsor accidently discovered a last-ditch measure for such emergencies. If used infrequently, and only in extreme cases, it generally proves 100 percent effective. (Using it every week on everyone would destroy its power.) A seventh grade boy developed into an absolute monster in the junior high group. A triple threat at every meeting, he endangered group order, sponsor sanity, and the physical safety of other youth. One Sunday evening, the sponsor was striding down a hallway toward the youth wing. He rounded a corner inches away from an eighth-grade girl falling on her face on the tile floor. Eddie had deftly tripped her in one of his frequent plays for attention.

Trying to make a quick getaway from his potential felony, young Eddie collided with the sponsor's stomach. Frustration finally exceeded controllable limits. The sponsor grasped Eddie by the shoulders and pointed him forcefully toward an empty classroom. The summit conference started in a typical manner, with the sponsor expressing concern about Eddie's attitude. But Eddie wasn't responsive to this approach. Jumping to his feet, he said with a scowl, "Well, I'll just go home."

But as Eddie turned toward the door, the sponsor was quicker. With a firm hand on each shoulder, he stooped eyeball to eyeball and said with even greater firmness, "That's fine, Eddie. But let me make it very clear that if you go home, I'm going with you. We'll sit down and talk to your parents about this. I want to see how *they* feel about your behavior. So you go ahead and make up your mind. We'll do it either way you want to. I'm quite willing to talk either place."

Eddie turned pale and looked blank for two seconds, then decided he wouldn't go home. Sitting back down, the conversation resumed in quite a different climate. That moment produced a total and permanent turn-around in Eddie's behavior with the group.

10. Involve parents at points where they can help. Have the pastor write a letter to all parents during late August. Invite them to a meeting during the Sunday school hour—junior high parents one Sunday and senior high the next. (Holding the meeting on a weeknight means many parents won't show up. But few can think of a good excuse for Sunday mornings.)

What should the pastor do at this meeting? First, sell them on the value of the evening program. Some parents think, "The kid goes to Sunday school on Sunday morning; why should he go on Sunday evening?" But when an authority figure like the pastor describes its value, they say, "Oh, I never thought about it that way." So tell them what makes youth groups important:

- a. They involve different goals and methods than Sunday school.
- b. Young people get something here which they get no place else in church life.
- c. The learning is experience-centered rather than content-centered.
- d. Fellowship and shared experiences have more impact than content-centered learning alone.
- e. These experiences prepare them for service on church boards and committees when they become adults.
- f. Organizational and leadership skills learned here improve their adjustment in all life's group situations.

Secondly, introduce the sponsors and brag on them. Express appreciation for their service this year. Help parents develop confidence in the sponsors' leadership and ability.

Thirdly, ask for the parents' cooperation. "This program cannot possibly succeed without your support. We need your help at several points. One is transportation. Many junior high youth don't get to evening functions because nobody will bring them. Since they can't drive a car yet, they stay home. Another place we may need your help is on trips. Some of you may occasionally be asked to drive cars for the group."

A special point for junior high parents: "We all know that junior high kids often resist new experiences because of shyness and sensitivity. 'Naa, I don't want to go to that,' is heard frequently from this age group. But after they participate in that activity, they often like it. So I want to urge you to help us in a way that only you can help. See that little Johnny gets to the first *four* youth meetings. Overlook all his complaining and groaning as a partial result of his age level. Just deliver the body to the church for the first four meetings. Give us a chance to get him involved and interested. If we haven't succeeded by that time, forget it. Let him drop out."

Fourthly, sign parents up for the snack supper. Pass a calendar around, asking two couples to volunteer for each Sunday evening. This solves the meal problem for half the year in five minutes. Always ask two couples, not one. If only one couple has the dinner duty, what happens if they go out of town that weekend? Who do they call? The sponsor or the pastor, that's who. And these busy people end up scrounging for someone to fill in. But *two couples* provide a built-in backup. In emergencies, they call each other.

The couples often decide between themselves that both will furnish food but only one will bring it to the meeting. That's OK. Let them feel good about being smart enough to work that out. You have accomplished your main objective—protecting the sponsors from the meal burden. They have enough to do without that extra load.

Mimeograph a big stack of 4″×6″ postcards. Each Monday morning one of the sponsors mails this reminder card to *both* of the couples:

Dear _____ ,
Just a reminder that this Sunday evening (date)_____
is your time to serve the snack supper for the youth groups. There will
be approximately (number) _____ of people present to
eat. Please plan to serve the food at 6:00 P.M. and remain for cleanup
afterward. The other couple helping you with this is (names) _____ .
We appreciate your willingness to assist us.
Sincerely,
Jane Sponsor

As well as eliminating all refreshment headaches, this system produces other fringe benefits. Parents actually *see* twenty or fifty kids milling around the church on Sunday evening. This strengthens their positive feelings about their church. "We really have a great youth program," they often tell their friends afterward. And that firsthand observation communicates enthusiasm to friends and other members like no other public relations device you can get.

11. Meet at the same time every week. Few successful groups meet less frequently than once a week. Nor can a group meet at six o'clock this month, five-thirty next month, and then change to Wednesday nights the following month. Time habits determine more personal choices than we suspect. What would happen if you switched the time of Sunday morning worship three months in a row? Confusion, attendance decline, and irritation. No, the clock rule isn't just a kid thing; it's a human thing. Break it and it breaks you.

Long weekends like Thanksgiving, Christmas, and New Year make exceptions to this need for utter regularity of weekly meetings. Because of family outings and the holiday air, few groups can sustain activity during these periods. Or if the school system takes a week off in the spring, you can't meet then. But otherwise, never cancel meetings except for floods, fires, or death of a sponsor.

12. Meet at the same place every week, preferably the church. The church building atmosphere is positive for almost everyone. Thus, nobody stays away because they don't like the person hosting the meeting. Above all, don't rotate the meeting from house to house each month. The resulting confusion kills attendance.

13. Balance your meeting time content. You must meet the needs of many different kinds of youth at many different ages and stages. Assume that "kids are all alike," and you plan for failure. Some youth possess a strong need for Bible study. Others hate study; they want recreation all the time. Most enjoy both, but not as a constant diet. Effective youth groups which continue to attract large numbers of youth therefore run a balanced meeting schedule. Surface appearances vary between groups, but a little prospecting always uncovers five basic elements in their meeting time content.

Eliminate one or two of these five, and your group generally falls apart.

a. Recreation: Playing together helps build interpersonal relationships; so don't classify it as "just goofing off."

b. Business Session: This interaction provides a learning experience not possible in Sunday school. Every Christian must learn how to co-operate with other church members. The business meeting, regardless of how chaotic, furnishes that educational possibility.

c. Study: Don't overload the circuits with study, but don't underesti-mate the need for it. All youth do some complaining about the study, re-gardless of what material you use. They must keep up an antiserious (sometimes antireligious) front before their peers. But don't take all that griping and moaning seriously and throw out the study. If you do, the group will fall apart. Parents of those who drop out will quote their teen-agers as saying, "Well, I just quit going; we never really did anything anyway. I have other things to do besides go down there and fool around."

d. Worship: This may not consume more than five minutes of the entire session. But it relates to the whole as importantly as the little hand on a big clock. Ecumenical endeavors among adults frequently fail because the constituent groups try to relate only by talking together or working together. They never meet as a worshiping community. The same prin-ciple applies to youth work.

e. Eating: Food is the glue that sticks the whole program together. Why do we have fellowship dinners for adults? Food contains more than calories. Sharing a meal opens the gate to deeper psychological and spir-itual communication. The early Hebrews wrote their legal contracts by cutting a piece of meat apart and eating together. Their word for covenant, *curath,* means "cut a covenant." They literally "cut a contract" and ate it together. When Jesus established a rite to help followers remember him, he used a meal for the basic elements. The highest point of the worship service in many denominations still involves eating this symbolic meal together. What do we do at family reunions? We eat. What do we do when faced with a complex business problem? Take the client to lunch.

Successful youth groups use various models to provide this common meal experience. Here's how one church does it: The junior and senior high groups both meet at 5:00 p.m. each Sunday (in different parts of the building). At 6:30, the two groups come together to eat. Combining the two groups for meetings would wreck both groups. But letting them eat together increases attendance in both groups. Why? For one thing, the older junior high girls are attracted to the high school boys (probably because their maturity levels are approximately the same at these de-velopmental stages).

How to handle the meal? In small churches, parents can do it in rota-tion. One large congregation handles it like this: All the youth groups meet at 5:00 P.M. (In this particular church, that involves five different groups covering all ages between first grade and high school.) Then, at 6:30, all the groups meet together in the fellowship hall for a snack dinner. One Sunday evening they have hot dogs (along with chips and a dessert like ice cream bars). The next Sunday evening they have hamburgers (with identical or similar accompaniments). This rotation repeats toward eternity without variation. The meal costs only forty cents per person, so kids can eat there cheaper than at home. And with the meals exactly identical, volunteer cooks can easily take turns producing it. Since this occurs prior to the Sunday evening service in that church, many adults eat there too.

A sample meeting time pattern containing the five basic ingredients needed in every meeting: Start with recreation. Good old American tradition saves the good stuff until last. "Eat your spinach first and then you can have the cherry pie." But if you start with a recreation like volleyball or touch football on the lawn, miracles begin to happen. The boys start showing up early. And you avoid fifteen minutes of confusion while waiting for everyone to arrive (especially the ones who drag in late hoping to miss the study).

Starting with thirty minutes of recreation also uses up excess energy. By wearing the kids down a little, the sponsors may have a chance of beginning even. After the fun and games, move to the business session. Some still show a little hyperactivity from recreational adrenaline, but business meetings generally run wild anyway. Next comes twenty minutes of study; perhaps more at some meetings, but generally not. Don't try to stretch attention spans beyond their snapping point. Even adults seldom tolerate more than a twenty minute sermon. Then add five minutes of worship. Food comes last, putting the final layer on a reversed Oreo cookie package: You pull them in on time with recreation. They look forward to eating at the end, so nobody leaves early. And you slip the nutritious, but more bland, stuff into the middle.

14. Provide leadership opportunities for many youth. Elect officers more than once a year, perhaps at the change of school semesters. This allows more youth to experience office holding. As well as teaching leadership skills, it stimulates anticipation in the group. "I didn't get president in the fall, but maybe I will the next time." In large groups of fifty youth, a committee system spreads responsibility and increases leadership involvement among more kids. One committee plans recreation, another study, etc. But most groups of fifteen or less need to use a "committee of the whole bunch." The entire group plans and decides everything together.

15. Coordinate sponsor planning between various age groups. Hold a planning session for sponsors of all age groups about August 1. Give them basic training for their work, covering the material in this chapter. Most sponsors begin with zero skill levels. You could let them learn the hard way—by experience—but that takes about five years of making mistakes. And most of them won't hang in there that long. Without training, they give up and fall out at the end of the first year or the first month.

At this first sponsor meeting, brainstorm and outline broad calendar plans for the year. Then about every three months in small churches (monthly in large congregations) all sponsors from all age groups should meet together. Some churches call this a Youth Work Council; others

100

a Youth Ministry Council. This allows groups to coordinate future plans—so the senior highs and junior highs don't schedule a bake sale on the same day.

16. Understand the needs of various age groups. Junior highs: Generally shy. In some cases, to the opposite extreme (an attempt to cover up shyness?). Busy trying to fit in by the way they dress, by group acceptance, by mental ability. Fearful of looking inadequate. Very sensitive to criticism. Great need for approval. Eager to assert themselves if they can excel in the activity. Like to participate more than to compete—competition brings fear of failure (unless it is group competition rather than individual competition). A time of enormous adjustments. Behavior patterns change radically, and daily, sometimes hourly. Leaders never know what to expect. A transition time through which no human being should be required to pass and which no parent should have to observe. Those who sponsor this age group deserve a medal for bravery, sometimes a purple heart. The only positive thing about the period—those who go through it usually get over it. Sponsors who keep that in mind sometimes retain their sanity.

Senior highs: Need a spirit of esprit de corps. Very conscious of peer acceptance—thus, fashions like hair and skirt length count even more than with adults. For the most part, able to handle adult situations. But maturity levels of different individuals vary radically. Some show adult reasoning and emotional levels; others act like seventh graders. Some yo-yo back and forth—mature this week, immature the next—mature at meetings, then immature on a trip.

At which grade level should you promote junior highs to senior high? According to the way your local school system divides them. Any other approach makes youth feel out of place and encourages dropouts. Only in the tiny church with a total of just four or five youth can these age levels meet successfully together. (Here, a family spirit negates normal group dynamics.) But in larger groups, the emotional, mental, and numerical age spans just can't be bridged. The youngest members feel overwhelmed with ideas beyond their emotional reach. The oldest members feel bored and put down when relating to too youthful youths.

17. Teach missions-benevolence giving through youth work. The group should decide in early fall how much they will give to church benevolent causes. Let the entire group wrestle with the percentage. Will they give 10 percent of the group income to outreach causes? Will they give 15 percent, 20 percent? To what causes will this money go, a children's home, overseas missions, world hunger, a missionary? When these youth become adults on a church board several years later, they won't ask, "What do we have mission giving in the budget for anyway?"

18. Select appropriate study materials. Some sponsors, like some Sunday school teachers, think that the "right" material works like a magic wand. Wrong! Groups rarely fail due to inadequate curriculum content. Most groups crash for one or both of two other reasons: The leaders don't understand basic principles of youth work; or, they lack the personality makeup required for relating to kids. Good study material can, however, help good sponsors make a good program better.

Publishing houses produce an almost unlimited cafeteria of printed materials. Unlike an earlier less ecumenical era, many of these instantly interchange among churches. Denominational leaders now encourage this smorgasbord approach to curriculum as never before in history. "Get the material which works best for you from anywhere you can," say many Christian education experts.

You and a bit of imagination can home grow some study materials. One group arranged with a Jewish rabbi to visit the synagogue in a nearby community. Since the Jewish sabbath begins at sundown on Friday, their services occur on Friday evening. The rabbi felt honored to receive a visiting church group. His evening sermon spoke eloquently about the basic beliefs of the Jewish faith. Afterward, the Jewish congregation invited their Gentile visitors to stay for punch and cookies. Junior and senior high youth attended together, plus many adult drivers and a few interested parents. That night taught them more about the Hebrew religion than their previous ten years in Sunday school.

Should the youth take responsibility for the study, or should the adult sponsors do it? At the junior high level, most groups experience zero luck with a steady diet of youth leading the study. With senior highs, results vary. Groups which experience consistent good luck with study generally use one adult sponsor for it. That person usually has an interest in teaching, plus the ability to get on youth wavelength. He or she uses a variety of study approaches. Do what works best for your group. Don't let other leaders in other churches make you feel inadequate because you don't do it their way.

19. Solve the sponsors' babysitting problems. Many churches limit their own recruitment pool by overlooking the babysitting needs of young adults. If the church hires a babysitter for Sunday morning, try to use the same one on Sunday evening. Sponsors can then feel the security of having their children cared for by someone familiar. (Parents ill at ease about childsitters don't make good sponsors, and certainly not long-term ones.) Tell the prospective sponsors, "We appreciate you giving your time, and we want you to know that we will furnish a babysitter at the church nursery for your own youngsters."

You can organize the babysitting several other ways—all of which work equally poorly. "Couldn't you get older people to sit at the sponsors' homes?" some penurious soul will inquire. But what if the sitter is ill, out of town, or wants to visit a sick aunt? Sponsors can't show up at the youth meeting. And what if the sponsors don't like this particular sitter? How can they possibly say to a *volunteer* that they don't like him or her? They might have to resign as sponsors in order to get loose without hurting someone's feelings.

Another poor method uses grandmothers to take turns babysitting at the church. Bad news. Not all grannies are equally sweet, loving, and understanding. Then too, babies don't enjoy exposure to ten different sitters. They need the sameness of one person with whom they (and their parents) can feel secure. And a different person coming each Sunday evening opens the possibility of *nobody* showing up. Illness, confusion, or scheduling foul-ups always afflict volunteer staff more than those paid to work.

20. *Hang in there*. A bishop who gets frequent requests for good advice to young pastors always says, "Hang in there!" Print that in triplicate if you try to support, supervise, or do youth work.

After a big horse race, the owner of an expensive mare asked his jockey why he hadn't ridden through a hole that opened up on the final turn. "Sir," the jockey replied wearily, "did you ever try to go through a hole that was going faster than your horse?"

Many leaders get that feeling when working with youth programs. But in spite of the challenges and stresses, these activities provide enormous opportunity for influencing young lives. Paul's line to the Corinthians applies nowhere more accurately than to youth work. ". . .we are ambassadors for Christ, God making his appeal through us" (2 Corinthians 5:20). So hang in there.

"Why a Pastoral Relations Committee?"

8 Happiness Beyond the Honeymoon

Fielding a Winning Pastor-People Team

John and Sarah have a great marriage. After five years, the future still looks sunny in their relationship.

Harry and Phyllis filed for divorce this week. Neither knows for sure what went wrong. But something did. "I'm simply not happy anymore," Phyllis says.

"It really doesn't matter that much to me," says Harry. "I'm tired of the hassle."

What made the difference between these two couples? Answered in an oversimplified way, John and Sarah meet most of each other's emotional needs. But Harry and Phyllis don't.

Pastor-people unions show marked similarity at this point. When the pastor meets most of the congregation's spiritual, emotional, and traditional needs, they stay happy. When the parishioners meet most of the pastor's needs, he stays around. If either's needs go unmet, relationships deteriorate and effective ministry diminishes. One or both sides start thinking divorce.

How can these mutual needs be reorganized, so that relationships reach optimum levels? In some churches, key leaders take it upon themselves to make sure their new pastor does well. During his first few years, they shape his ministerial knowledge through close personal relationships. They know that the church cannot succeed unless their pastor succeeds. So they work hard at seeing that he does.

But many ministers find no such lay persons in their new parish. They encounter instead a group of people so fearful of conflict that they withhold even the smallest criticism. (They may tell their friends, but never him.) Thus, the new pastor tries to achieve a "good marriage" with little or no direct communication from the new partner.

Called by various names in different denominations (and structured in various ways), the pastoral relations committee solves this problem for many congregations. When designed and operated according to successful principles, this communication tool brings big dividends to any congregation: 1) It helps the pastor do a better job; 2) It helps the lay leaders do a better job; 3) It helps the people whom God calls both leaders and pastor to serve; 4) It adds years of effective ministerial tenure to each pastorate; 5) It stacks mountains of additional satisfaction in the shepherd's personality; and 6) The pastor finds his best continuing education opportunities coming from teammates in his own parish.

Leaders who wish to develop an effective pastoral relations committee have a choice of three different models or designs. In denominations where the congregation uses a pulpit committee to call their pastor, the following model has demonstrated itself extremely practical: After the call of a new minister is completed, the board chairman appoints the pulpit committee as a pastoral relations committee. (If the pulpit committee was larger than five or six people, he appoints only part of them.) This committee schedules four meetings annually. Meeting less than this produces the disastrous feel of an annual inquisition committee. Good pastor-people communications can never develop in that once-a-year atmosphere.

How can you sell a church board on the value of a pastoral relations committee? Mimeograph the following six points and hand every board member a copy. Then read them aloud and illustrate each briefly. Most people immediately see the sense of the idea.

Why a Pastoral Relations Committee?

1. To help the minister get a more accurate picture of how his congregation sees him than he might receive informally.

2. To allow the minister to express opinions regarding how well the board is fulfilling its responsibilities to him.

3. To establish goals for both pastor and congregation in the coming year.

4. To isolate areas of conflict or disappointment which adversely affect working relationships.

5. To clarify expectations on both sides of the pastor-people team.

6. To provide an additional tool for the board to use in setting future compensation.

Why appoint the old pulpit committee instead of a totally new group? Because they have already developed a comfortable group relationship by working and traveling together. They *like* the new pastor. And he *knows* they like him. After all, they just hired him. And they know that if he doesn't succeed, it publicly reflects on their judgment in selecting him. This ready-made rapport allows him more frankness with them (and they with him) than any other persons in the church. Thus, he won't get as paranoid if one of them says, "Now preacher, thirty-five minutes is a bit long for a sermon, don't you think?" He knows the person is seeking to be constructive rather than picky. The pastor would have to spend one or two years with any newly appointed group in order to reach that level of trust.

Form such a committee only at the beginning of a ministry, before any conflicts can arise. Making the appointment at the pastorate's midpoint, or when a minister is under fire, can make things worse instead of better. It creates the appearance that leaders are taking their leader in hand so they can smack his hand. Do not, of course, set up the committee without the knowledge and consent of the new pastor. But most ministers readily agree to the idea. They know it can protect them from much heartache and increase the quality of their ministry.

Don't wait until a good reason arises for calling the first meeting. (That's like waiting for your first heart attack before you get a physical.) By then, the problem has grown too big to deal with effectively—and the emotional bias of some committee members might stifle open communication. Nor should the committee ever invite the pastor's spouse to these meetings. The husband or wife may adopt a defensive stance when people criticize their spouse—adding a complex group dynamic which muffles communication channels.

The format of the quarterly meeting should run something like this: First, follow the rule that everyone must speak, including the pastor, each time an opinion is requested on anything. Nobody can remain silent. Secondly, the chairman goes around the room asking each person to name at least one good thing they see happening in the church right now. This starts the meeting on a positive note. Otherwise, it can easily deteriorate into an unconstructive gripe session. By starting this way, the pastor always gets some positive strokes, creating a climate of warmth. Thirdly, the chairman asks each person to mention one problem area that may need attention. Some extraneous matters will always come up here. "The thermostat is never set high enough in our classroom," someone will say. But try to accept everyone's feelings without judging them or putting them down. If necessary, refer them or their problem to another appropriate committee. Fourthly, keep pointing the discussion toward constructive suggestions about how to solve particular problems.

By this point in the meeting, the committee members will have entered a free-floating discussion. They have no real authority over the pastor, except the power of opinion and caring communication. But since they aren't under the pressure of bringing things to a vote, feelings flow more openly and naturally. Creativity comes to the surface more readily here than in the pressure cooker of heated board meetings.

At the first quarterly meeting after launching the committee, little of significance may transpire. But that happens at the first meeting of most new groups. And these "practice sessions" prepare members for working together well when more complex matters arise (usually about one year after the ministry begins).

A Pastoral Relations Committee

Denominations which use the appointment system (or those who don't wish to use their former pulpit committee) will find the following alternative design useful:

The Purpose of the Committee: The primary function of a pastoral relations committee is to aid the pastor (staff) in performing an effective ministry by advising him concerning conditions within the congregation that affect the relationship between pastor and people, and continually interpreting to the people the nature and function of the pastoral office.

Methods for Accomplishing the Committee's Purposes: The committee should provide opportunities for counseling on all matters pertaining to the minister's relationship with the congregation. These would include priorities for the use of time and skills, pulpit supply, proposals for salary, travel expense, vacation, continuing education, housing, and all other matters relating to the effectiveness and well-being of the minister and the minister's family. It should make recommendations to the church board for the necessary time and financial assistance for the minister's attendance at such schools or institutes as may serve intellectual and spiritual growth. In cases where a parsonage is furnished by the church, the pastoral relations committee should devote at least one meeting per year to an on-the-spot inspection of the parsonage in order to prepare recommendations to the church board regarding needed repair and/or improvements.

A pastoral relations committee should consist of not fewer than five nor more than nine lay persons, including at least one young adult and at least three women. The members, including the chairperson, should be appointed annually by the church board upon recommendation by the church board chairman. Where a minister is serving more than one congregation at the same time, there should be a pastoral relations committee with at least one representative from each congregation. In churches where there is a multiple staff, the committee shall relate to the entire staff, but individual meetings should probably be held with each pastor. It should elect its own secretary, if one is desired. It should meet at least four times each year. It should be able to be called into session at other times by the request of the bishop, the district superintendent, the pastor, the board chairman, or the committee chairman. Guidelines for how to conduct evaluation sessions in order to pinpoint specific problems and maximize communications in the committee can be obtained from most bishops or judicatory representatives.

The committee should meet only with the knowledge of the minister. It should be able to meet with the bishop or the district superintendent without the minister being present. But when the minister is not present, he or she should be informed prior to such a meeting and immediately thereafter be brought into consultation either by the committee or by the bishop or judicatory representative. In the event that only one congregation of two congregations being served by the same pastor has concerns which it wishes to share, its member(s) on the pastoral relations committee should be allowed to meet separately with the minister or bishop or all together as required.

Congregations in some denominations find it extremely practical to use their key spiritual leaders (called elders) to perform the functions of a pastoral relations committee. If this model is used, four factors are crucially important in making it work: 1) Regular frequent meetings of the elders; 2) Shared responsibilities; 3) Sharing of honest feelings with each other (you obviously can't share feelings with people you never meet with); and 4) Daily prayer for each other (we can't stay irritated with people for whom we pray every day).

The collegiality developed by this atmosphere shields pastors from their most debilitating enemy. Not the long hours, though protestant ministers in the United States average sixty-five hours a week. (But since many pastors are workaholics anyway, that doesn't really bother them.) Not the low pay, though pay often stays far below that of bricklayers and truckdrivers. Not the middle-of-the-night calls, though these too frequently steal sleep. No, *loneliness* outranks all of these as a reducer of ministerial zip. Pastors do much emotionally draining work. They deal with many problems which they can't discuss with anyone. They receive much criticism and become the emotional garbage dump for many unhappy people. Without strong team support they easily see greener grass in other congregations, or even other vocations.

As well as helping the pastor's development, such regular sharing prevents many congregational frictions. One district minister says that lay leaders often come to him saying, "We are having trouble with our pastor."

When that happens, he always asks, "How often do your elders meet?"

Ninety-five percent of the time the layman replies, "We only meet when we have a problem to discuss."

The district minister always responds, "Well, you have a problem now, don't you?"

And the lay leader says, "Yes, but this problem is too big now. I don't think we can talk about it in a meeting."

When leaders frequently meet together and pray together, communication lines stay open. They talk through little problems, preventing their growth into big unresolvable problems.

Whatever system is used, no pastor grows to greatness without a group of concerned colleagues. He needs people who care about him, communicate with him, and pray for him. Have you ever played on a good ball team, a clicking team which wins close games? If so, you never forget that feeling. You would like to play on such a team again. With this kind of spirit among church leaders, ministers grow rapidly in maturity and effectiveness. Without it, they tend to mediocrity and eventual disillusionment.

9 Creating Better Camel Construction Crews

Organizational Leadership

Seven years before 1492, Columbus sailed for the port of Palos in the southwestern corner of Spain. By May of the following year he finally obtained an audience with Queen Isabella, a Catholic monarch. The Queen referred his plea for funding to a committee, a *church* committee. After considering this matter for five years, the committee submitted a report. "Impossible, vain, weak, and worthy of rejection," they wisely concluded. His request was then referred to a second committee. They said that his idea was sound but would be far too expensive. The queen finally overruled both committees and gave Columbus permission to make the trip during which he discovered America.

Stories like this help us poke fun at organizational work. "A camel is a horse organized by a committee," we quip. "If God had assigned a committee the job of getting the Israelites out of Egypt, they'd still be there." And we set cute little signs on our desks which read, "For God So Loved the World, That He Didn't Send a Committee."

But in spite of the partial truth in all these gags, good leaders know they must take organizational work seriously. Few congregations elect a Moses for board chairman. And they call ordinary mortals as minister, not Jesus. So they must use normal procedures to make decisions and get things done. Paul lists administration among the spiritual gifts. Along with

111

prophets and teachers, God calls some people to organizational leadership (1 Corinthians 12:28). And he had good reasons for reminding the church at Corinth about that. A well organized worship committee might have saved him the stress of writing them that first scalding letter.

The New Testament gives at least two good reasons for sharpening our organizational skills: Firstly, ". . .all things should be done decently and in order" (1 Corinthians 14:39). Some members complain that "Our church is overorganized." Probably not. Many churches suffer from *poor* organization, but seldom from *over*organization. Secondly, good administration helps ". . .to maintain the unity of the Spirit in the bond of peace" (Ephesians 4:3). In a well organized congregation, things get decided by groups, not by autocratic individuals. This may mean that things get decided a little more slowly. But it also means that members feel more positive about the final decisions. So they ultimately spend less time fighting about church work and more time doing it. Autocrats can act quickly, but people eventually respond to them with some kind of revolutionary war.

Avoiding the Sandtraps

Even the most experienced leaders frequently overlook the following axioms. These apply to every committee and planning group in the church.

1. Program like a cafeteria, not a one-dish meal. A cook who points an accusing finger at patrons who don't take *every* dish in the serving line would look pretty silly. And don't expect everyone to participate in everything that happens in the church. Even the tiniest congregation consists of several smaller groups of people. Each group, because of differing interests and needs, derives benefit from different phases of church life. Some ladies love women's groups; others can't stand them but will gladly teach a Sunday school class or sing in the choir.

2. Rearview mirrors make poor windshields. Focus on tomorrow's possibilities, not yesterday's problems. In Iowa, the farm barnlots get almost impassable during the winter. In order to deal with the deep mud, many dairy farmers wear "gum boots." Even then, walking out across a lot presents hazards. Sometimes when you start to take a step, your foot pulls out of the knee-high boot. Then you must carefully put your foot back in the boot and retrieve it from the mud. Some church members operate like that. No matter what you discuss, they are hung up in the past. Every new program proposal gets blocked by a recording of some past disaster that occurred in that department of church life. If you ask them when that terrible thing happened, they may tell you, "I guess that must have been in 1943."

3. Dream the impossible dream, but don't take up residence in it. An opposite of the rearview mirror board member is the one who gets hung up in the *future*. He always says to every proposal, "We can't do that now.

112

Perhaps we can do that when. . .When we get a little bigger we can. . . When we get a little more money. . .When we get something. . . ." This group also accounts for many frustrating board meetings. Add them to the rearview mirror types and there aren't many people *here* tonight. Nobody is present in the present.

4. *Don't pass the ball to people in the bleachers.* Leaders often blame their problems on what inactive or lazy members don't do. This game, called "Ain't It Awful," provides a subtle substitute for positive thinking and action. After the committee plays an evening of it, each member goes home feeling much better about himself. But nothing has been accomplished. Face it: You have no power over inactive members. You can bad-mouth them, but you can't control them. You can only decide what you plan to do with those who attend.

5. *Bring new programs to birth, but don't murder old ones.* A seminarian takes a student church in rural Indiana. The young adult class in that congregation now totals three persons—all of whom are women over age seventy. They meet in a large room that could easily seat thirty. The men's class now contains four people, the youngest of whom is sixty-five. Short on Sunday school rooms, the church needs to start a new class. Logical conclusion: Combine these two classes. So the young minister tells the members they will do this starting with next Sunday. Result: He almost loses his job. Class leaders complain to the elders, "The preacher is trying to run the Sunday school." Avoid trying to terminate old programs. Let them die a natural death. If participants don't decide to drop them, the program still hasn't become invalid to *them.*

6. *Buy a new dress occasionally; don't patch the old one forever.* The membership committee meets to plan a fall program. "What did we do last year?" someone invariably asks. Someone else starts remembering. Another member suggests some slight changes to improve last year's model. If used exclusively, this approach automatically blocks all creative thinking. Boredom is the root of much evil in church life. Occasionally, try something totally new.

7. *Goal setting is never enough.* The goal setting fad swept through most denominations during the 1960s. "Long-range goals, short-range goals, intermediate goals," became the motto at all levels. But most churches acted as if setting the goal automatically guaranteed its achievement. No specific times were set for evaluating their progress. By the end of the year, most members couldn't even remember what the goals were.

With every specific goal, always set a specific board meeting or committee meeting date to evaluate your progress toward its achievement. "Are we moving toward the goal? If not, why not? Do we need to change our methods? Is the goal still valid? Do we need to scrap the goal altogether?" Time span between these evaluation sessions should never be more than three months. Individuals who set strong personal goals for themselves usually evaluate their methods daily. But a church which doesn't set a *specific date* for this probably won't do it at all.

113

8. Build the future on your successes, not your failures. Many churches try to improve themselves by continuously analyzing their weak spots. Such navel gazing often produces a reverse effect. They constantly feel like a failure. What if you met a friend once a week to discuss the question, What is the matter with me? Each week you tell the friend what you think your flaws are. And he agrees that these are your flaws. Every week you meet and do the same thing again. What would happen? Either you would become very perfect or very depressed, probably the latter. Some church committees follow this exact procedure. And they depress each other toward failure instead of perfection.

A better question: What specific things are we doing well—probably better than most other churches? What is our greatest strength? Building on these, and improving them still more, usually generates more enthusiasm and growth than constant Sherlocking for weaknesses.

Leadership in the Smaller Congregation

"I need some help, preacher." Frank Symington, a young oil company engineer, had dropped by his pastor's office on impulse. His real destination this Wednesday morning is a drill rig south of town. Frank looks discouraged. He feels worse. Two months ago he eagerly said, "Yes, I'll be glad to serve as membership chairman." Now he can't get his committee to function. Nobody shows up for the meetings. He can't understand why. Unfortunately, Frank's pastor can't help him much. He listens sympathetically, but he doesn't know what to suggest.

Leaders in many small churches face similar organizational dilemmas. The denomination hands them functional committee methods designed for large churches. But trying to apply these systems to the small church usually fails. Then the leader, who usually can't think of a good alternative method, says to himself, "Something must be wrong with me. I don't know how to do it. I suppose I need to work harder at it." So he works harder, but that doesn't work either.

At the next stage, the chairman blames the people in that particular congregation. *They are just lazy,* he thinks. *They don't care what happens to their church. They just aren't serious about their Christian faith.* After that phase, he begins to say to his wife, "If *they* don't care, why should I?" So he gives up trying to get his committee to function. He starts saving time and frustration by making most of the decisions himself. That quickly gets him into hotter water. "The chairman tries to run everything," people mumble. "He should have cleared that with the committee!" When that static starts, the hard-working leader begins to wish he had never accepted the chairmanship. Sometimes he acts on that feeling and resigns.

The following system works well for setting up a practical democracy in smaller churches. Lay leaders can immediately understand and implement it:

114

Organizational Alternatives
to the Functional Committee System

The small church hardly has enough leaders to staff the chairman slots, much less people the committees. Most committee meetings therefore find only two or three persons showing up. And they spend most of their time feeling depressed and trying to figure out how to get better attendance at future committee meetings—rather than actually doing committee work.

A council system works much better for the small church (and some large ones). This can be launched without changes in the church constitution. Simply appoint all the chairmen whom you would ordinarily appoint to head committees. But instead of holding committee meetings, hold monthly council meetings. The board chairman or vice-chairman usually presides. As the meeting proceeds, the council chairman asks each individual chairman around the table to bring up matters which they need to discuss and plan for in their section of church life during the next two or three months. For example, at the October meeting the worship committee chairman may need to discuss the date and features of the special Christmas service. While the worship committee chairman has the floor, all other chairmen become members of his committee for that few minutes. This ensures a democratic decision regarding what needs to be done. It also ensures that when an event or plan is put into operation most key leaders of the church already know about it and will therefore support it. And if the matter is a policy decision which needs to be cleared with the church board later, it will easily go through. Many key leaders of the board have already considered it in the council meeting. This radically reduces friction and conflict in the board meetings of small congregations, who often try to function as both board and committees for the church.

In small congregations, because of the natural flow of the year into different aspects of church life, some committees will consume more time than others during one particular month. Thus, the worship committee might take up a great deal of time at the April meeting, but almost no time at the May meeting. If necessary, this rotation can be systematically structured into the calendar so that more time is given to one or two committees at one particular monthly meeting, and then to other committees at other monthly meetings. Because of this rotation, the council always has plenty to discuss, but meetings rarely need to take more than one hour.

Following the council meetings, the committee chairman may wish to appoint a particular person or persons from the congregation to execute specific tasks or events. Their responsibility continues for the duration of that event only. This allows specific talent to be used in specific ways and involves the whole membership in various activities throughout the year. More people, rather than less, can often be included in church work. Many people would much rather help on a specific project than serve on a committee for an entire year.

Where does the minister fit in this structure? He participates in the council. This provides a perfect position from which to ask questions and generate ideas regarding each section of church life. Since he is not chairing the meeting, he can more easily ask questions and give nondirective leadership. He may find it helpful to collect mail and ideas for each committee in a file folder during the month. Then prior to the meeting, while the chairmen are gathering, he can distribute pertinent mail and talk briefly with each chairman to whom he wishes to give particular suggestions about matters that need to be decided. This allows him to do effective administrative work in a minimum amount of time. It also saves the chairman the embarrassment of forgetfully leaving important pieces of mail at home, thus preventing them from being discussed.

Having this council meet five times each year is more effective for some very small congregations than having a monthly meeting. Several churches have found the following pattern beneficial: Hold the first meeting in September—the logical beginning of the church programming year; hold the second meeting in November—which gives time to prepare for Christmas events; hold the third meeting in January—the start of the year; hold the fourth meeting in March—which generally gives plenty of time for Easter preparation; hold the last meeting in May—to prepare for summer events. This procedure eliminates the need for meeting during months when meetings are hard to hold anyway. Few churches want to have committee meetings in December—they are too busy with Christmas. Few committees meet effectively in the summertime—everybody is too busy with vacation, summer work, and recreation.

The above procedures provide a good alternative between two bad extremes—either having the board try to do all the committee business during the board meeting; or having small committees which meet irregularly and rarely function effectively when they do meet.

Improving the Officer Election Process

How should you elect officers in order to create an effective leadership team? Very carefully, especially the top leadership. Paul warns us to elect as key leaders only those proven in middle-management (1 Timothy 3:10). In this testing process, candidates should meet qualification standards in four areas:

1. Regular Worship. The nominating committee, meeting together on a balmy August evening, tries to finish quickly. Two members say they need to go home and mow their lawn. So they look at the slots that need filling and somebody says, "Why don't we put John in? He's a real nice fellow."

Someone else says, "That sounds pretty good."

Another member says, "But he doesn't come very often."

"Yes, he comes quite a bit," the first person protests.

A week later the membership secretary tells the minister, "Why did they nominate John? He has only attended church three times during the whole year."

Why would you elect someone to help manage a church who attends less than 25 percent of the time? Would a corporation do that? Hardly. They would consider such action irresponsible and potential fiscal suicide. And how can a nominating committee avoid this mistake unless they set some minimum standard? And how can they function objectively without consulting the keeper of attendance records?

2. Regular Financial Support. Stewardship dipsticks spiritual depth in one of the most measurable ways. People who care about Christ support his work. If they don't, their commitment can logically be questioned. One young man quit the ministry with despair and feelings of failure. Later, he learned that three close friends gave the church no financial support whatever. All had served in key board positions. No coach would go to the world series with players who don't believe in baseball. Responsible nominating committees try to protect church teams from that irony. They consult the financial secretary before nominating people for high offices (not to determine amounts, but to check on giving consistency).

3. Spiritual Qualities. Some churches select people as elders because they look like elders. Those who reach fifty and have white hair automatically become candidates. One church elected a wealthy banker as a vestryman, feeling that he would add prestige to their community image. This is approximately like a medical school which gives out degrees to people who look like Dr. Marcus Welby.

4. Personal Attitudes. A green persimmon personality can sour a whole barrel of good church leaders. Some people can't help using negative, caustic, and critical language. When their mouth opens, their negative case goes in gear. But nominating committees can avoid putting them on important boards and committees. No church would consciously employ a minister with acutely negative attitudes. They know that these rub off on people and inhibit church vitality. So why throw away that obviously true criterion when selecting officers?

In some denominations, middle-management officers are called deacons (from Acts 6:1-8 and 1 Timothy 3:8-13). At this level, many congregations err by using the appointment as a motivational tool. They elect someone as a deacon hoping to encourage him toward increased church activity. Occasionally, this works. New responsibility produces better participation levels. In general, however, the principle generates ecclesiastical disaster areas. Follow it for three years and you develop an unfunctional church board. Many officers won't show up for board meetings. Those who do come spend much time pondering why nobody comes to the meetings. They start feeling bad about themselves because they assume, "Something must be wrong with us!" Then they start devising strategies to get more people to attend. The whole psychological atmosphere of the church swings to downbeat.

A personnel manager with a manufacturing firm says, "Appointing someone as a deacon hoping it will make him a good church member is ridiculous. That's exactly like my promoting a bad employee in the hope that it will make him a good employee. That may work occasionally, but not often. In most cases it demoralizes the rest of the employees—makes them think that advancement doesn't come by merit but by accident.''

A few simple steps can reduce the frustration of low performance officers. First, instruct the nominating committee. Most committees meet and come up with names to fill the slots. Recognize this as a fatal mistake—getting people to fill slots. The committee thinks Joe might do it, so they go talk to Joe and say, "We need someone to fill a spot as deacon. You don't have to do much. There is really nothing to it."

This approach sets the church up for a dwarf leadership crop. What they really said to Joe was, "Any dummy can do this, and you are any dummy. Why don't you do it?" Will that inspire Joe to responsible performance, wanting to attend meetings regularly? Why should it? The committee told him that he doesn't have to do much. So he takes them seriously. When he gets into office, he performs exactly the way they told him he should.

A nominating committee does far better by agreeing on qualifications *before* they start thinking of names. This introduces quality control into the selection process. The roulette wheel procedure changes to a talent search. Then when they talk to candidates, they can say, "Our committee has used a high set of standards to select deacons this year. It is very important that these officers attend board meetings and worship regularly, give regular financial support to the church, and take their duties extremely seriously. We think you are the type of person who will do this."

One congregation helped their nominating committee to strengthen standards by adding the following to their constitution and by-laws: "The nominating committee shall have at its disposal worship attendance records and a list of those church members who have been consistent in stewardship. It shall also review the biblical qualifications for these offices found in Paul's letters to Timothy." This mandate protects committee members from the social pressure to select at random instead of by qualifications.

Some constitutions create automatic problems by saying, "At least sixteen deacons will be elected each year." So the committee is forced to mindlessly cast about for sixteen warm bodies. Saying yes to the request becomes the only standard for election. Some small churches are thus forced to choose officers who don't even attend church. This system ensures general irritation about poor officer behavior for years to come— until the persons chosen in that manner are no longer in office.

Changing one sentence in their constitution has helped one church eliminate this problem. It now reads, *"Not more than* sixteen deacons shall be elected each year, depending on availability of qualified candidates." Better to have six active deacons than sixteen goof-offs. Electing low performance people to offices is like putting up a billboard that says, "These offices are unimportant."

One congregation nominates first time deacons for only one year instead of the usual three. Then at their orientation session after election the pastor says, "This is the first term of office for some of you. Since you have been elected for only one year, you may feel like you are on trial. That is the truth. You are. As you know already, we elect people on very high standards. And we expect them to meet these high standards of board meeting attendance, regular worship participation, and consistent stewardship. You have been carefully selected because we believe you will strive for excellence as a church officer. Of course, if you do not meet these standards, you will not be reelected." Delivered in a positive and somewhat humorous way, new officers appreciate this challenge.

People in that church now *aspire* to these offices. After the word finally got out that "not just anyone can be elected," attitudes reversed. Instead of hoping that the nominating committee won't ask them, they strive to qualify for election. So setting higher standards has ironically increased the number of potential candidates rather than reducing them. Changing the congregation's mind-set took about three years. But the results made the trip worthwhile.

An annual education effort at the time of officer nomination helps in this transition process. Members have usually derived their low estimate of deacon and elder performance from observing those elected in recent years. So changing their expectation standards requires concentrated reeducation efforts. Along with constitutional changes, pastors can help promote attitudinal shifts by repeatedly lifting up the biblical yardsticks for measuring church officers.

Every denomination interprets the exact meaning and function of New Testament leaders differently. Scholars now more accurately understand the meaning of the Greek word *diakonos*, noting that exactly the same word has been translated into English as a female officer in one place and a male officer in another. (Compare Romans 16:1 and 1 Timothy 3:8.) This perception now allows many churches to appoint women to serve as deacons. Regardless of denominational interpretation, periodically dipping the congregation into biblical texts eliminates many false ideas. Paul's officers were clearly not authority figures who directed the minister's work from the sidelines. Nor were they selected from the ranks of Christmas and Easter attenders.

One congregation aids this never-ending educational process by printing the following material in their newsletter each year.

Scriptural Qualifications for an Elder

1 Timothy 3:1-13; Titus 1:5-9; 2:1-8; 1 Peter 5:1-9

1. Blameless, without reproach (Titus 1:6, 7; 1 Tim. 3:2).
2. Husband of one wife (Titus 1:6; 1 Tim. 3:2).
3. Having children in subjection (Titus 1:6; 1 Tim. 3:4).
4. Not self-willed (Titus 1:7).
5. Not soon angry (Titus 1:7).
6. No brawler, no striker (Titus 1:7; 1 Tim. 3:3).
7. Not greedy, but good steward (Titus 1:7, 1 Tim. 3:3).
8. Given to hospitality (Titus 1:8; 1 Tim. 3:2).

9. Lover of good men (Titus 1:8).
10. Just (Titus 1:8).
11. Holy (Titus 1:8).
12. Self-controlled (Titus 1:8).
13. Sober minded, temperate (Titus 1:8; 2:2).
14. Holding to the faithful Word (Titus 1:9; 2:2).
15. Able to teach (Titus 1:9; 2:2, 3; 1 Tim. 3:2).
16. Orderly (1 Tim. 3:2).
17. Grave (Titus 2:1; 1 Tim. 3:4).
18. Not a novice (1 Tim. 3:6).
19. Not given to much wine (Titus 2:3).
20. Good reputation with outsiders (1 Tim. 3:7; Titus 1:6).

Scriptural Duties of the Elder

1 Timothy 3:1-7; Titus 1:5-9; Acts 20:17-35;
1 Peter 5:1-4; 2:25; Ephesians 4:11; James 5:14

1. Take heed to yourself (Acts 20:17, 18).
2. Take heed to all the flock (Acts 20:28).
3. Take heed to the Holy Spirit (Acts 20:28).
4. Feed the church (Acts 20:28).
5. Watch over the flock (Acts 20:31).
6. Protect the flock (Acts 20:29, 30).
7. Help the weak (Acts 20:35).
8. Give (Acts 20:35).
9. Tend the flock (1 Peter 5:1, 2; Ephesians 4:11).
10. Exercise the oversight (1 Peter 5:2).
11. Not lording it over the flock (1 Peter 5:3).
12. Be examples of the flock (1 Peter 5:3).
13. Follow the example of Jesus (1 Peter 5:4; 2:25).
14. Call on the sick (James 5:14).
15. Teach (sinners and Christians) (Titus 1:9, 1 Tim. 3:2).

Scriptural Qualifications for a Deacon

1 Timothy 3:8-13; Titus 2:6-8; Acts 6:1-6

1. Grave (sober-minded) (1 Tim. 3:8; Titus 2:7).
2. Not double-tongued (1 Tim. 3:8; Titus 2:8).
3. Not given to much wine (1 Tim. 3:8).
4. Not greedy (1 Tim. 3:8).
5. Holding the mystery of the faith in a pure conscience (1 Tim. 3:9; Titus 2:7).
6. Deacon must be proved (1 Tim. 3:8).
7. Blameless (1 Tim. 3:10).
8. Husband of one wife (1 Tim. 3:12).
9. Ruling children and own house well (1 Tim. 3:12).
10. An example of good works (Titus 2:7).
11. Of good report (Acts 6:3).

12. Full of the Holy Spirit (Acts 6:3, 5).
13. Full of wisdom (Acts 6:3).
14. Willing to serve (work) (Acts 6:1-3).
15. Full of faith (Acts 6:5).

Duties of a Deacon

The very word means "servant." The first deacons, selected by the church in Jerusalem, were chosen to administer to the needs of the widows of the congregation. The New Testament does not speak in terms of "office" or "position" as much as it does of the "work" and "service" of those who are chosen for these duties.

Deaconesses

"I commend to you our sister Phoebe, a deaconess of the church at Cenchreae, that you may receive her in the Lord as befits the saints, and help her in whatever she may require from you, for she has been a helper of many and of myself as well," wrote Paul to the church at Rome (Romans 16:1-2).

To the church at Phillipi, Paul made this plea: "I entreat Euodia and I entreat Syntyche to agree in the Lord. And I ask you also, true yokefellow, help these women, for they have labored side by side with me in the gospel together with Clement and the rest of my fellow workers, whose names are in the book of life" (Phillippians 4:2-3).

It is commonly assumed that such an order existed from apostolic times. Second and third century Christian literature has reference to deaconesses. In one of these, there is an excellent summary of the functions of a deaconess: 1. To assist at the baptism of women; and 2. To visit those who are sick, and to minister to them in their need and to bathe those who have begun to recover from their sickness.

Promoting Peaceful Coexistence in the Congregation

Most churches strive for peace and unity. But exactly how do you achieve that state? The following list of factors determines the presence or absence of this invisible commodity. Find most of them present, and members feel warm toward each other: "We have a great church. The future looks bright." When several of these factors are absent, members fuss a lot: "Things are running off in all directions. Several people are unhappy."

1. A temperamentally positive pastor. Ministers tend to attract birds of similar feather. And they tend to do a taxidermy job on members who are already in the church. A positive pastor molds a positive church in two or three years. A negative, critical one remolds members in that direction within two or three months.

2. Optimistic lay leaders. We complain about air pollution hanging over our cities. But a worse kind of negative smog clouds many congregations. When they gather for coffee at the local drug store, they share nothing but bad news. "Did you hear what the preacher did to Jerry? Did you hear what a stupid thing they are putting in our new building?"

Such information quickly produces a negative public image for that church. Jesus says we are defiled, not by what goes into our mouth, but by what emerges (Matthew 15:11). That applies to churches too. It isn't, what goes in the front door on Sunday morning that destroys them; it's what comes out of the mouths of members in idle moments. Moses followed a pillar of cloud by day and a pillar of fire by night (Exodus 13:21). Many modern congregations are surrounded by a cloud of pessimism. And it leads them, not to the promised land, but through forty more years of wilderness.

How do you correct a negative smog bank in a church? Just like you control a hot furnace with the thermostat on the wall. When someone starts a hypercritical monologue, notice how quickly everyone in the group tends to follow suit. Like sheep flocking over a cliff, they jump at the chance to add a negative comment. Some time when that happens, do a little field testing. Intentionally follow the first negative statement with, "But he really has some good qualities too." Then illustrate one of these. In most groups, people will start emulating you instead of the negative person.

3. Willingness to experiment with programs. If the board or committee can't agree on an idea, why not try it for three months? See how it works. Meet for an evaluation session at the end of that period. That way, nobody loses. Reality, not personality, decides the issue.

4. Congregational involvement in decision making. As much as possible, those affected by the decision should help make the decision. People need to know that their opinions count.

5. Effective communication networks. You haven't communicated with the membership until you say it three times in three different ways. Newsletters furnish the least effective communication tool. Announcing it from the pulpit ranks next. Personal letters are the next rung up the ladder. Phone calls exert more power than letters. Going to their home and saying it face-to-face stands at the top of the list. You communicate with almost everyone that way—except for a few people who are preoccupied with personal problems. But some combination of three of these methods is much better than any one alone. Then too, people make decisions about some things slowly. They may dismiss the church picnic at the first hearing. But the second time it hits their ears, they decide to go.

6. Openness to discussion and disagreement. All social systems must provide a means for the expression of differing opinions. Restrict these from coming out in meetings and they go underground—into the private world of thought and gossip channels. Restrained in this way, contrary viewpoints change to hostility, which eventually explode in some public way—like the Spanish Civil War, the Watts riots, or the taxpayer revolt.

Damming up the flow of opinions doesn't eliminate disagreements; it postpones them. Effective leaders encourage feelings to come out in meetings, so they won't have to face them later in some dark alley.

7. A sense of timing about making changes. The timing gear in a car fires spark plugs at the right second in the right cylinders. Churches need that too. One congregation feels proud about the new parsonage they built this spring. If attempted three years ago—before the sanctuary note was paid off—they would have divided in anger. Confucius says, "Leaders who pressure congregations to premature decisions because of their own ego needs usually get mud in their eye."

8. Willingness to learn all the facts. Postpone decisions until all the evidence comes in, especially until everyone *thinks* all the evidence is in. "Jim, why don't you check on that and report back to us at the next meeting? Then we will know for sure how to proceed."

9. Warm feelings between officers and members. The way people feel about each other always counts for more than what they accomplish together. If members sense that the officers don't really care about them as persons—they only want to *run* the organization successfully—friction eventually fractures all the good work attempted.

10. Continual focus on worship. Churches exist to help us center our mind and life on God. Leaders who concentrate only on good social inter- action of members—like the "I'm OK, You're OK" fad of the early 70s—generally fail. The health of our horizontal relationship with other people grows out of our vertical relationship with God. Jesus says that the first commandment is ". . .you shall love the Lord your God with all your heart. . ." (Mark 12:30). Trying to put the second commandment ahead of the first is like pulling an engine with the caboose.

11. Respect for the opinions of all age groups. Some churches won't listen to the ideas of anybody less than eighteen years old. One congre- gation refused to install a coke machine in the kitchen. They said the broken bottles and pop spilled on the tile floor would create a mess. Each of the adults who made that decision had a coffee cup in hand. (They always drank coffee at their committee meetings.)

12. Quick inclusion of new members in church activities and structure. Some small congregations do this *too well.* They elect someone as property chairman before he gets dried off from baptism. Big churches tend to the opposite extreme. Unless new members possess aggressive, outgoing per- sonalities, they slip through the organizational cracks. People need signals of acceptance from their new family. If they don't get these, they feel silently hurt. This sometimes leads to hostility about some minor matter which serves as a pop-off valve for their pain. Or, they just fade away to the inactive list—another way to reject being rejected.

13. An active effort to help the community. Churches exist to serve their community as well as their members. For God so loved, not just the church, but the world. A church living only for itself soon dies of spiritual strangulation. Stinginess is never next to godliness; it's next to extinction.

Identifying Your Leadership Type

What is your leadership style? You probably don't know. Your rationalizations provide a neat protective shield from most bad news about yourself. But your humility may protect you from the good news too. Read the following descriptions of the three basic leadership styles found in all churches. Then test yourself with the forty-two questions.

1. The Autocratic Leader: He decides most group policies. After all, he is the chosen leader. He determines techniques, procedures, and group activities one at a time. Future steps are left vague because he hasn't decided them yet. And he doesn't want to confuse the group with too many projects at once. He appoints all the committees, sets time and place of meetings, and determines what work shall be done. He gives his own personal praise as a sign of appreciation by a benevolent leader. He also gives needed criticism because he is the leader and needs to give proper guidance.

2. The Passive Leader: He maintains a total "hands off" position. His leadership is like a bowl of gelatin. It may quiver a little if jarred, but mostly it just sits there. Allowing complete freedom for the group to formulate all its own policies, he takes no part in discussions or decision making. He offers advice only when requested. He doesn't assign work or set time deadlines. He maintains no pressure toward achievement of goals. He maintains a passive attitude, neither praising nor criticizing except when asked. He enters a disagreement only in times of personal danger to himself.

3. The Democratic Leader: He encourages the group to discuss and decide policies. He helps formulate goals, points out alternatives and consequences, supplies technical advice when needed, but permits a group choice. He gives members freedom to work with whomever they choose and to divide tasks as they see fit. But he maintains pressure toward goal achievement and against disorder. He reacts as if he were a member of the group. He tries to be objective and fair in praise and criticism. But he doesn't hold himself up as the final judge of everything.

Now place a "D" before each statement which you think describes a democratic leader. Place an "A" before items which you think describe an autocratic leader. Place a "P" before those which you think describe a passive leader.

1. _____ I give credit for achievements.
2. _____ I ask for indefinite postponement of decisions.
3. _____ I offer my service.
4. _____ I allow complete freedom.
5. _____ I offer no advice.
6. _____ I defend myself.
7. _____ I talk much about "I," "me," and "mine."
8. _____ I admit my errors.
9. _____ I give no praise.

124

10. _____ I confirm the views of others.
11. _____ I maintain a hands-off policy.
12. _____ I give credit for good attributes.
13. _____ I accept obligations.
14. _____ I seek praise.
15. _____ I invite participation.
16. _____ I assign no work.
17. _____ I determine most of the details.
18. _____ I maintain no pressure toward group achievement.
19. _____ I lecture the group.
20. _____ I give examples.
21. _____ I assume an "it's up to you" attitude.
22. _____ I offer no materials or ideas.
23. _____ I offer suggestions.
24. _____ I demand cooperation.
25. _____ I am impartial but not uninterested.
26. _____ I discourage people.
27. _____ I take no part in the discussion.
28. _____ I encourage people.
29. _____ I threaten people.
30. _____ I ration materials.
31. _____ I am passive.
32. _____ I seek and use advice.
33. _____ I take no part in decisions.
34. _____ I mention alternatives.
35. _____ I neither guide nor direct.
36. _____ I am partial to group members.
37. _____ I ask the group to choose.
38. _____ I directly refuse requests.
39. _____ I offer no criticism.
40. _____ I don't care what happens.
41. _____ I participate like most other group members.
42. _____ I demand approval of my acts.

Characteristics of the democratic leadership style are listed in numbers 1, 3, 8, 10, 13, 15, 20, 23, 25, 28, 32, 34, 37, and 41. Autocratic leaders are described in numbers 2, 6, 7, 12, 14, 17, 19, 24, 26, 29, 30, 36, 38, and 42. Passive leaders are pictured by numbers 4, 5, 9, 11, 16, 18, 21, 22, 27, 31, 33, 35, 38, 39, and 40. Which style did you have the most difficulty in identifying? Does that tell you anything about yourself?

Now go back and lay a paper over the answer column on the left. Make an honest check mark every time you think the sentence describes *you*. If you have the nerve, exchange lists in a group of leaders who know each other well. Have your friend mark all the blanks which he or she thinks describe you. See if you can catch yourself using a particular pattern in your next committee meeting.

Does it really matter what type of leader you are? Emphatically, yes, yes, yes, yes, yes, raised to the power of infinity. The various leadership types produce specific results in committees. Democratic leaders increase participation and attendance at meetings. People appreciate being part of their group. They feel worthwhile around such leaders.

The autocratic leader gets things done. But attendance diminishes and creativity dies. People discover that their opinions don't make any difference anyway. So they stay home. Some become apathetic. Others grow inwardly angry at the leader. Sometimes they get mad at themselves for letting him run things. But since they don't want to make a fuss, they don't say anything. Instead, they may retaliate by exploding in anger over some minor detail in church life. Or they may withdraw from participation in everything, just to prove to the leader that they really do matter.

The passive leader raises the frustration level of all concerned. The organization runs like a stringless kite. At times it soars to great heights of discussion, but who knows where it will come down? Committee members want to accomplish something, but can't. They don't get angry quite so soon as with the autocratic leader. In fact, the passive leader may be such a nice guy that they can hardly fault him. But eventually they will. They finally get irritated with membership in a do-nothing organization. So they too eventually drop out. Who wants to attend meetings where nothing ever happens?

One expert describes a good leader like this: "But the wisdom that comes from heaven is first of all pure and full of quiet gentleness. Then it is peace-loving and courteous. It allows discussion and is willing to yield to others; it is full of mercy and good deeds. It is wholehearted and straightforward and sincere" (James 3:17 TLB).

Lao-Tse, an oriental sage writing in 600 B.C., sums it up this way:
"A leader is best
When people barely know he exists
When his work is done, his aim is fulfilled
And they will all say, 'We did this ourselves'."

Bibliography

Chapter 6
The Association of Theological Schools in the United States and Canada, "Readiness For Ministry" 1975, Vol. I, p. 75.

Chapter 7
Lubbockview Christian Church Newsletter, Lubbock, Texas. Article by Bob Coleman, pastor. March 9, 1977.